The
Vietnamese
Americans

The Vietnamese Americans

Hien Duc Do

THE NEW AMERICANS
Ronald H. Bayor, Series Editor

Greenwood Press
Westport, Connecticut • London

Library of Congress Cataloging-in-Publication Data

Do, Hien Duc, 1961–
    The Vietnamese Americans / Hien Duc Do.
        p.   cm.—(The new Americans, ISSN 1092–6364)
    Includes bibliographical references (p.   ) and index.
    ISBN 0–313–29780–0 (alk. paper)
    1. Vietnamese Americans.   I. Title.   II. Series: New Americans
(Westport, Conn.)
    E184.V53D6   1999
    973'.049592–dc21   99–22706

British Library Cataloguing in Publication Data is available.

Library of Congress Catalog Card Number: 99–22706
ISBN: 0–313–29780–0
ISSN: 1092–6364

First published in 1999

Greenwood Press, 88 Post Road West, Westport, CT 06881
An imprint of Greenwood Publishing Group, Inc.
www.greenwood.com

Printed in the United States of America

The paper used in this book complies with the
Permanent Paper Standard issued by the National
Information Standards Organization (Z39.48–1984).

10 9 8 7 6 5 4 3 2 1

To our daughter,
Meiko Mai Huong Flynn-Do
and to our son,
Koji Hiep Duc Flynn-Do.
You have brightened our lives more than you will ever know.

Contents

Series Foreword

Oscar Handlin, a prominent historian, once wrote, "I thought to write a history of the immigrants in America. Then I discovered that the immigrants were American history." The United States has always been a nation of nations where people from every region of the world have come to begin a new life. Other countries such as Canada, Argentina, and Australia also have had substantial immigration, but the United States is still unique in the diversity of nationalities and the great numbers of migrating people who have come to its shores.

Who are these immigrants? Why did they decide to come? How well have they adjusted to this new land? What has been the reaction to them? These are some of the questions the books in this "New Americans" series seek to answer. There have been many studies about earlier waves of immigrants— e.g., the English, Irish, Germans, Jews, Italians, and Poles—but relatively little has been written about the newer groups—those arriving in the last thirty years, since the passage of a new immigration law in 1965. This series is designed to correct that situation and to introduce these groups to the rest of America.

Each book in the series discusses one of these groups, and each is written by an expert on those immigrants. The volumes cover the new migration from primarily Asia, Latin America, and the Caribbean, including: the Koreans, Cambodians, Filipinos, Vietnamese, South Asians such as Indians and Pakistanis, Chinese from both China and Taiwan, Haitians, Jamaicans, Cubans, Dominicans, Mexicans, Puerto Ricans (even though they are already U.S. citizens), and Jews from the former Soviet Union. Although some of these people, such as Jews, have been in America since colonial times, this series concentrates on their recent migrations, and thereby offers its unique contribution.

These volumes are designed for high school and general readers who want to learn more about their new neighbors. Each author has provided information about the land of origin, its history and culture, the reasons for migrating, and the ethnic culture as it began to adjust to American life. Readers will find fascinating details on religion, politics, foods, festivals, gender roles, employment trends, and general community life. They will learn how Vietnamese immigrants differ from Cuban immigrants and, yet, how they are also alike in many ways. Each book is arranged to offer an in-depth look at the particular immigrant group and to enable readers to compare one group with the other. The volumes also contain brief biographical profiles of notable individuals and a short bibliography of readily available books and articles for further reading. Many contain a glossary of foreign words and phrases.

Students and others who read these volumes will secure a better understanding of the age-old questions of "who is an American" and "how does the assimilation process work?" Similar to their 19th- and early 20th-century forebears, many Americans today doubt the value of immigration and fear the influx of individuals who look and sound different from those who had come earlier. If comparable books had been written 100 years ago they would have done much to help dispel readers' unwarranted fears of the newcomers. Nobody today would question, for example, the role of those of Irish or Italian ancestry as Americans; yet this was a serious issue in our history and a source of great conflict. It is time to look at our recent arrivals, to understand their history and culture, their skills, their place in the United States, and their hopes and dreams as Americans.

The United States is a vastly different country than it was at the beginning of the twentieth century. The economy has shifted away from industrial jobs; the civil rights movement has changed minority-majority relations and, along with the women's movement, brought more people into the economic mainstream. Yet one aspect of American life remains strikingly similar—we are still the world's main immigrant-receiving nation and, as in every period of American history, we are still a nation of immigrants. It is essential that we attempt to learn about and understand this long-term process of migration and assimilation.

Ronald H. Bayor
Georgia Institute of Technology

Acknowledgments

Many people have helped in many ways to enable me to complete this book. I owe my deepest thanks and sincere gratitude to the Vietnamese Americans who shared their lives, dreams, and hopes with me. This book would not have been possible without their stories and insights. Our community will be stronger and better as a result of their hard work, dedication, and commitment. Sincere thanks to Professor Ronald H. Bayor, series editor, and Jennifer K. Wood and Wendi Schnaufer at Greenwood Press for their suggestions and editorial skills throughout this project. I owe a special thanks to my graduate advisors—Dick Flacks, Rich Appelbaum, and Bill Bielby—at the University of California, Santa Barbara, for their encouragement and guidance through graduate school. Part of this research was made possible through the support of a predoctoral grant from the Minority Fellowship Program of the American Sociological Association and a dissertation fellowship from the University of California. Portions of this book were taken from my dissertation "The New Outsiders: Vietnamese Refugee Generation in Higher Education." A special thank you to Steve of Steve G. Doi Books for providing books and other materials for part of this research. Many thanks as well to my students at San Jose State University who have taught me how to be a better teacher. Thanks to my wife Sarah Akemi Flynn for all her emotional support, intellectual challenge, and continued love throughout my career. As usual, thanks to my parents Kim Cuc and Hanh for their love. All my love to my brothers and sisters.

Chronology

1627   French influence begins in Vietnam when Alexander De Rhodes, a missionary, adapts Vietnamese language to Roman alphabet.

1787   French military intervene in Vietnamese political affairs.

1861   French military forces capture Vietnam.

1863   French influence spreads to Cambodia.

1887   France creates Indochina, which includes Vietnam, Laos, and Cambodia.

1940   Japanese troops occupy Indochina (Vietnam, Laos, and Cambodia) during World War II.

1945   World War II ends. France attempts to return to and occupy its former colonies in Indochina.

1954   The French are defeated by the Viet Minh, led by General Vo Nguyen Giap at Dien Bien Phu.

1954   Geneva Conference. Vietnam is temporarily partitioned under the Geneva Accord. There is to be a national election in 1956 but it never takes place. The United States helps evacuate one million northern Vietnamese Catholic refugees to the south.

1954   Ngo Dinh Diem becomes premier of the Republic of Vietnam (South Vietnam). Ho Chi Minh becomes the leader of North Vietnam.

1963   In a coup d'etat South Vietnamese Premier Ngo Dinh Diem and Ngo Dinh Nhu are assassinated.

1964   The Gulf of Tonkin incident. President Johnson asks Congress to pass the Gulf of Tonkin Resolution. The resolution passes and thus begins the "formal" involvement of the United States in Vietnam.

1965   U.S. combat troops arrive in South Vietnam.

1967   After a series of military coup d'etat, Generals Nguyen Van Thieu and Nguyen Cao Ky become respectively, the president and vice president of South Vietnam.

1968   Tet Offensive. Vietnamese communists temporarily occupy South Vietnam, including the United States Embassy, for a few hours. The number of U.S. soldiers stationed reaches its peak.

1973   Paris Peace Agreement signed between North and South Vietnam. This ends the U.S. military involvement in Vietnam.

1975   Vietnamese Prime Minister Thieu resigns on April 21. On April 30, North Vietnam defeats South Vietnam and captures the country. More than 100,000 Vietnamese flee their country as refugees.

1980   Passage of the Refugee Act of 1980, which defines the refugee status and requires the federal government to provide assistance to the refugees. Ethnic Chinese are forced to leave Vietnam.

1987   Amerasian Homecoming Act allows Vietnamese born of American fathers to immigrate to the United States.

1994   United States lifts trade embargo against Vietnam.

1

Introduction

"Vietnam,"[1] is deeply embedded in the American psyche. It is an ambivalent word that appears repeatedly in popular culture and historical consciousness. Hundreds of films and books have emerged about the Vietnam War. Most of these films and books are about the American experience in Vietnam. However, Vietnam is much more than that. It is a country that has a long history, is rich in culture and deep in customs and traditions. Since the end of the Vietnam War in 1975, thousands of Vietnamese refugees and immigrants have called the United States of America their home. This book is part of their stories; it is also a part of my family's story.

In the early hours of April 25, 1975, I was hurriedly awakened by my mother. Uncle Hau, my father's younger brother who was a member of the Diplomatic Corps of Vietnam to the Philippines, had just returned home to arrange for our evacuation. He had risked his life by returning to Saigon (now Ho Chi Minh City) to try to get members of his family to freedom. We had a couple of hours to ready ourselves for the long journey that awaited us. We were told to pack as little as possible and to bring only the absolute necessities. Obediently following these instructions, I managed to pack a pair of pants, a couple of shirts, some underwear, and, without anyone's knowledge, my special stamp collection book.

As daylight approached and we began our journey, all of us were filled with a wide range of emotions, from excitement to fear, danger, and sadness. Despite our "official" document, we neither knew how we were going to exit Vietnam, nor where our final destination was going to be. However, we were among the lucky ones: those who were able to leave Vietnam on airplanes before the collapse of the Vietnamese government on April 30, 1975. On that day we became refugees without a country.

Vietnamese refugees arrived to the shores of America a little more than twenty years ago. Since then, many more have arrived and are now calling the United States their home. Vietnamese Americans have established communities in cities across the nation from New York City, to San Jose, California; trained a new generation of professionals; participated in the social, political, economic, and cultural life of America, and contributed to social problems facing our society. More importantly, we now have a new generation coming of age—a generation of Vietnamese Americans who were born in the United States and are now a part of the American mosaic in some urban cities.

Today, at a time when immigrants, both legal and illegal, are under severe attack; when the debate over multiculturalism and diversity is sweeping university and college campuses; when the effectiveness of bilingual education continues to be questioned; and when Affirmative Action is facing unprecedented setbacks, this book will focus on the trials and tribulations of a relatively new immigrant group to the United States: Vietnamese Americans.

GEOGRAPHY

Vietnam is located on the southeastern coast of the Indochinese peninsula (from 8 34'N to 23 22'N) and occupies about 329,566 square kilometers. The country is S-shaped, geographically broad in the north and south, and very narrow in the center—about 50 kilometers at the narrowest point. The coastline measures 3,260 kilometers, and the country shares 950 kilometers of border with China to the north, 1,650 kilometers with Laos to the west, and 1,150 kilometers with Cambodia to the southwest.

Vietnam is a country of tropical lowlands, hills, and densely forested highland, with level land covering no more than 20 percent of the total area. Three quarters of the country consist of mountains and hills, the highest of which is Phan Si Pan (also spelled "Fansipan,") at 3,143 meters, in the Hoang Lien Mountains in the far northwest of northern Vietnam. In the central highlands is the Giai Truong Son mountain range (Central mountains, or Annamite Cordillera).

Vietnam's two main cultivated areas are the Red River Delta (15,000 square kilometers) in the North, and the Mekong Delta in the South (60,000 square kilometers). The Mekong Delta, created by silt deposited from the Mekong River, is very fertile. About 10,000 square kilometers are under rice cultivation, making the area one of the major rice-growing regions of the world.

As a result of its geographical location and the wide range of differences in latitude, Vietnam has a diverse climate. Since the country lies in the Southeast Asian inter-tropical monsoon zone, the weather is determined primarily by two monsoon seasons. From May to October summer monsoons from the south greatly influence the weather in the North and South regions yet leave the central area dry as a result of the air-flow patterns. The weather in each region varies considerably and there are noticeable seasonal differences as a result of Vietnam's geographical location.

LANGUAGE

Vietnam was dominated by China for a long period of time, so the Vietnamese language was highly influenced by the Chinese writing system. As a result of the long Chinese influence, Chinese characters were primarily used in government documents, the educational system, literature, and other important official transactions. In time Vietnamese scholars desired to gain their independence from Chinese and to express themselves in a language of their own, leading them to develop a Vietnamese language for which they borrowed Chinese characters but combined them with Vietnamese concepts, sounds, ideas, and phonetic sounds. Thus came *chu nom*, or "vulgar" or "demonic" language, as seen by the Chinese. Even though characters in the new language looked similar to Chinese characters, they were different and distinct and were not understood by the Chinese. Although *chu nom* was popular with Vietnamese scholars and nonscholars alike, it was used primarily in popular literature and was not accepted as the official language by the Chinese, who insisted that their language remain as the only official language.

The current language used by most Vietnamese is *quoc ngu*, or national language. *Quoc ngu* was developed during the seventeenth century by Catholic missionaries from Europe. Alexandre de Rhodes, a Jesuit scholar and missionary from France working with other scholars romanized the Vietnamese language, which was then written in characters. He published a Vietnamese-Portuguese-Latin dictionary in Rome in 1651. As Vietnam became a colony of France, *quoc ngu* became the official language taught in schools. A series of campaigns to replace *chu nom*, with *quoc ngu* as the official language of Vietnam and to promote literacy throughout the country, resulted in *quoc ngu* becoming the official language in all government and nongovernment transactions in 1954.

Although *quoc ngu* became the official language in Vietnam, there remained three regionally distinct dialects in the country reflecting the three regions: north, central, and south. These regional differences represent both the particular regional history and cultural uniqueness of each region. The dialects also serve to maintain the people's emotional attachment to their regions, especially after their continual displacement throughout the country as a result of war. Similar to regional differences in the United States (northeast, west, south, midwest, and so forth), the bond between people from the same region in Vietnam is much stronger because Vietnam is a much smaller country. In fact, it is not unusual for a Vietnamese from the north to make fun of one from the south and vice versa.

Despite the fact that *quoc ngu* was romanized, Vietnamese has its own unique linguistic structure. The words are pronounced consistently the same, and the same letter represents the same sound. The most complex and perhaps most difficult aspect of the language is the tonal changes and the accent marks that are put over or under vowels. They illustrate the tone (or pitch) on which the word is to be pronounced. By placing different accent on different words, the meaning of the word is changed. As a result, it is difficult to read Vietnamese without the correct accents and tones because the meanings are easily altered. Since *quoc ngu* is derived from roman roots, the letters in the alphabet are the same with a few exceptions. For example, while a "D" without a bar in the middle (or stem) is pronounced similar to "z," with a bar in the middle, it is pronounced like a regular "d." Although there is no letter "z" in the language, there are many words that are pronounced as though there were a "z" sound. Additionally, many words are a combination of two words that have meaning by themselves and become a different word when combined. Further adding to the confusion are regional variations in pronunciation. A speaker from the North will pronounce "v" as a "v," while a speaker from the South will pronounce it like a "y."

COMMON FAMILY NAMES

There are about one hundred family names for Vietnamese people. However, only about a dozen are frequently seen. The most common last name is Nguyen. Other common last names include Tran, Ngo, Phan, Vo, Le, Dang, Do, Pham, Vu, Truong, Trinh, and Luong. Unlike name order in the United States, the usual order of Vietnamese names in Vietnam is: family name, followed by a middle name, and, finally, the given name. Take, for example, Ngo Van Minh. Ngo is the last name, Van is the middle name, and Minh is the given name. The middle name oftentimes designates gender. Females usually have "thi" (e.g., Ngo Thi Kim Cuc) as part of their middle name. In general, a Vietnamese family name does not have any meaning. However, parents usually choose their children's given name to describe the child's personality or out of respect for someone in the family. These names are usually combinations of two words that create the intended meaning when put together. As a result, Vietnamese given names frequently have meanings, such as Xuan Lan (Spring Orchid), Thu Cuc (Autumn Chrysanthemum), Xuan Son (Spring Mountain), and Do Quyen (Azalea). When inverted in the American system, such names lose their intended original meanings and thus become meaningless.

PEOPLE

The largest ethnic group in Vietnam, about 85 percent of the population, are ethnic Vietnamese. Although seen as a single ethnic group, Vietnamese are a mixture of different racial groups including Austro-Indonesian and Mongolian. As a result of many intermarriages between different ethnic groups throughout Vietnam's long history and continuous expansion to the South, many groups have been absorbed into a single Vietnamese group.

The rest of Vietnam comprises numerous different ethnic groups. The three largest are the Chams, the Khmer, and ethnic Chinese. The Chams are primarily found in central Vietnam. Originally from Indonesia, Chams are descendants of the Cham Kingdom, called Champa. Like other countries in the region, the Chams have been involved in many wars throughout their history. The Chams were finally defeated by the Vietnamese in 1471. Although absorbed into Vietnam, the Chams continued to maintain their own ethnic and cultural practices. They have created their own ethnic enclaves and live as a minority group in Vietnam. Currently, there is a Cham Museum located in the city of Da Nang in central Vietnam.

Another ethnic group in Vietnam is the Khmer group. Most Khmers live south of the Mekong River. Descended from the Khmer Empire, the Khmers trace their origins back to the Mons of Burma. Like other ethnic groups in the various regions, the Khmers were attacked and defeated by Thais in 1432 A.D. Following the aggressive social policies of Vietnam regarding ethnic minorities throughout its history, the Khmers remained a small and distinct ethnic group in the Mekong Delta.

The third largest ethnic group in Vietnam before 1980 were the ethnic Chinese. Prior to the forced mass exodus by the Vietnamese communist government, more than a million Chinese lived in the south of Vietnam, primarily in *Cho Lon* (Chinatown). As in most of Asia where Chinese have resettled, they dominated the economic and business life in Vietnam. Although many ethnic Chinese had been living in Vietnam for several generations, many chose to practice their Chinese culture as well as to maintain close ethnic ties with their homeland. Despite being an important part of Vietnam's economic infrastructure, there was a certain degree of distrust and resentment between Vietnamese and Chinese because Chinese were seen as not wanting to become a part of the Vietnamese society. Chinese were also resented because they were economically successful and tended to only help other Chinese. This tension and resentment culminated in their expulsion from Vietnam by the Vietnamese communist government in 1979 and 1980.[2]

RELIGION

Four philosophies and religions have shaped the spiritual life of Vietnamese people: Confucianism (*Khong Giao*), Buddhism (*Phat Giao*), Taoism (*Lao Giao*) and more recently, Catholicism. Collectively, Confucianism, Buddhism, and Taoism are referred to as *Tam Giao* or the Three Religion system.

Confucianism

Confucianism was founded by Confucius in China. Confucius was born in China around 550 B.C. He saw people as shaped by society and in turn shaping their society. He believed that since a people live in society, there needed to be a code of ethics to govern our social interactions. This code of ethics described an individual's specific obligations to family, society, and the state. Two of the central tenets of Confucianism are duty and hierarchy. Although there are different schools of Confucianism, the one found in Vietnam is heavily influenced by Han-Confucianism, as interpreted by Tung Chung Shu (179–104 B.C.). The most important ritual in Confucianism is that of ancestor worship. Most Vietnamese homes and businesses will have an altar dedicated to family ancestors. The altar is generally decorated with candlesticks, incense bowls, a flower tray, and a tablet or pictures containing the names of ancestors who have died in the last five generations. These altars are a constant reminder to the family members of their ancestors and the place from which they have come. On special occasions, such as *ngay gio*, the anniversary of a death, altars are filled with food, fruit, drinks, and flowers to pay special homage to ancestors.

Over time, beginning in the fifteenth century until the nineteenth century, Neo-Confucianism became the dominant influence. As Vietnam was defining itself, Neo-Confucianism was embraced by the Nguyen dynasty in an attempt to make it the foundation of national culture. Neo-Confucianism believed that the emperor alone, governing under the mandate of heaven, can speak on behalf of the nation with the powers of heaven and earth. Consequently, the emperor needed to be virtuous by acquiring education. When the sovereign is virtuous, he will be able to direct his functionaries and govern the people in a just manner and the country will be at peace. By 1802, Neo-Confucianism became the most important source for determining social values and proper social relationships in Vietnam.

Buddhism

Buddhism originated in India about 500 B.C., founded by Siddhartha Gautama Buddha. Siddhartha, born around the year 563 B.C., was a crown prince in India. As he witnessed the suffering of those around him, he abandoned his privileged lifestyle and went searching for a doctrine preaching human salvation. At the age of twenty-nine, he left the royal palace and wandered to the countryside. At thirty-five, while meditating at the foot of a tree, he received enlightenment as to the path of deliverance. Thereafter, Siddhartha traveled broadly and disseminated his doctrine, which became known as Buddhism and spread to many regions of India and other parts of Asia. Siddhartha died at the age of eighty.

Although there is no agreement on how Buddhism entered Vietnam (either through China or directly by sea through Indian traders), scholars agree that Buddhism in Vietnam is derived from India. There are Four Noble Truths taught by Buddha: life is suffering, suffering is caused by desire, suffering can be eliminated by eliminating desire, and to eliminate desire, one must follow the Eightfold Path of righteousness: understanding, purpose, speech, conduct, vocation, effort, thinking, and meditation. In general, Buddhism teaches that life is suffering. To end suffering, one must try to escape the endless birth-death cycle called reincarnation by following the Eightfold Path. Reincarnation is the belief that everyone has had many lives and will have additional future lives. A record is kept of one's total good and bad actions during these lives. This is referred to as the Law of Karma. Therefore, at the end of one's life, if all the good deeds outweigh the bad deeds, the immediate future life will be better than the current life. If not, the next life will be worse. This is reflected in the Buddhist belief in the sacredness of all life forms, including insects, other animals, and human beings. As one continues to live many lives and to acquire good Karma by following the Eightfold Path, one may eventually enter Nirvana, a state of oneness with the universe and the point where the endless cycle of reincarnation stops. Peace of the soul is thus attained. This is the goal of all followers of Buddha.

Taoism

Similar to Confucianism and Buddhism, Taoism arrived in Vietnam from China centuries ago. Taoism was founded by Lao Tse in China around 604 B.C. Although Taoism is contemporarily thought of as a religion, Lao Tse thought of himself as a philosopher. His philosophy focused on the idea of human being's oneness with the universe. The fundamental belief in Taoism is that since the laws of the universe and nature cannot be changed, one should not try to change them, instead, one should be content to live with them and to make the best of the situation under the circumstances. This philosophy was readily accepted by Vietnamese when Taoism was first introduced because it offered new explanations for human sufferings and encouraged people to accept their lot in life since there is nothing they can do to change it. Because of the long history of suffering that Vietnamese people had endured as a result of the many different wars, this philosophy offered an explanation for the harsh conditions that many people faced throughout the years.

Catholicism

Catholicism was introduced into Vietnam in the sixteenth century by missionaries from Spain, France, and Portugal. From the very beginning, Catholicism was discouraged and at times outlawed by the Vietnamese government. Since it was a foreign religion that had neither cultural nor historical roots in Vietnam, it was seen as a threat to the established structure of the society. On the other hand, the treatments and persecution of Catholic missionaries and Vietnamese followers by the Vietnamese government also served as pretexts for military intervention by France. Although there are many Vietnamese Catholics throughout the country, most are from North Vietnam, including many who became refugees in 1954 when the country was divided in half.

Minor Sects

There are two important minor religious sects in Vietnam in addition to the four major religions: Cao Dai and Hoa Hao. Both religions have been recently established in Vietnam and are confined to the rural sectors of the Southern Delta Region. Combined, these two sects have nearly three million followers.

Cao Dai

Cao Dai was founded in 1919 by Le Van Trung. He used a synthesis of different beliefs, including the teachings of Buddha, Jesus, Confucius, Lao Tse, and the French author Victor Hugo. The main headquarters is the Great Temple located in the city of Tay Ninh, about sixty miles from Ho Chi Minh City. One of the most outstanding features of the Great Temple is the Heavenly Eye. The Heavenly Eye is a naturalistic picture of a human eye and represents the omnipresence of Cao Dai.

Hoa Hao

Hoa Hao is a reformed Buddhist sect of the Theravada variety. It was founded by a twenty-year-old youth name Huynh Phu So in 1939 and is primarily concentrated in the southwest and the Mekong Delta. Huynh stressed virtue in one's daily conduct as the chief method of seeking salvation. Hoa Hao was not only a religious movement it was also a political movement since Huynh argued that both politics and religion were concerned with salvation. At the end of World War II, when the Japanese surrendered to the Allies, the sect refused to follow the communist leadership. Huynh Phu So was later killed by the communists, and his followers became opposed to the communists throughout the Vietnam War.

CULTURAL VALUES AND CUSTOMS

Family

The family is the most important of all social units in Vietnam. In contrast to the focus on individualism in the West, the close-knit family is the basic unit in Vietnamese society. "*Hieu,*" or filial piety, is one of the basic virtues. This refers to the idea of love, care, and respect that children give to their parents. This obligation is unconditional, even in the case of a parent who abandons the children or does not fulfill his or her parental duties. Children are taught this virtue from a very young age. The socialization process normally begins at home with the teachings from grandparents and parents. This educational process continues throughout a child's early years and is reinforced throughout all the social institutions. One of the most well known Vietnamese proverbs is "*Cong Cha nhu nui Thai Son, nghia Me nhu nuoc trong nguon chay ra. Mot long tho Me kinh Cha, cho tron chu hieu moi la dao con,*" or "The debt we owe our father is as great as Mount Thai Son; the debt we owe our mother is as inexhaustible as water flowing from its source. We must repay their debt in order to fulfill our obligations as children" (Huynh, 1988). In fact, a person who does not fulfill filial piety, "*do bat hieu,*" is sanctioned severely by members of the family.

The cradle of the traditional Vietnamese society was the village, the place that provided the individual with a sense of community and security in a potentially hostile environment. This, along with the importance of the family, created a network of extended kinship and family ties. In traditional Vietnamese culture, strong individuals in a family have an obligation to the weaker and less fortunate members of the family (or village). Every action of every family member reflects on the family, be it achievement or shame. There is a sense of obligation and of providing for the welfare of each and every member of the family. Everyone has to contribute to the well-being of the entire family. An individual who achieves fame at the expense of the family is discouraged and even sanctioned.

The family in Vietnam was also an extended one, unlike the typical "nuclear" family in the United States. The family traditionally was composed of three to five generations living in the same house, typically including parents, children, grandparents, and sometimes, unmarried uncles and aunts. The extended family acted as a source of mutual support and as an institution where individual problems and social conflicts could be resolved. However, the long history of multiple wars changed the basic structure of the Vietnamese family. Because many family members and individuals were killed during all the different wars, it would be difficult to maintain the expected ancient traditions and practices. Although the family structure fundamentally remains an extended one, in urban areas particularly, the family is limited to three generations: grandparents, parents, and children.

Vietnam also a has patriarchal system where the man, or husband, serves as the head of the family. He takes care of money matters and is responsible for providing for the family. The woman is in charge of the affairs in the home and raising the children.

Education

For Vietnamese, education is revered. To achieve high education is the way to achieve high status and to be considered successful in the society. A proverb that suggests the importance of the scholar class is, "*Mot nguoi lam Quan, ca ho duoc nho,*" or "A mandarin can help all his relatives" (Huynh, 1990). In ancient Vietnam, the emperor was assisted by a corps of functionaries called "*quan lai,*" the mandarinate. The mandarinate had two orders, the civilian mandarinate, "*quan van,*" and the military mandarinate, "*quan vo.*" The civilian order was much more prestigious and therefore entrance much more sought after by means of the educational system. A mandarin was someone who, because of his success as a scholar, served as an official in the government. As a result, it was not unusual for people to want to pursue an education and to take, and hopefully pass, the very difficult series of examinations to become mandarins. The order of respect in society reenforces this set of beliefs, "*Quan, Su, Phu,*" or King, Teacher, Parents.

Class

Since Vietnam is greatly influenced by Confucianism, Buddhism, and Taoism, there is a prescribed social hierarchy in the amount of respect given to different classes in society. This social hierarchy includes the scholar class at the top of the pyramid, followed by cultivators (or farmers), manual workers (or laborers), merchants, and finally, soldiers.

The scholar class includes primarily people who are educated, such as mandarins, teachers, physicians, and those who were students who attempted but did not pass the extremely difficult series of national examinations. In ancient Vietnam, the scholar class was small—only 2 to 3 percent of the entire population. As a result, high performance and educational attainment by an individual always brings pride to the entire family. Members of this class are generally highly respected by the entire society for their education, knowledge, and wisdom. Members of this class were also primarily responsible for advising the emperor in managing and maintaining the affairs of the country in ancient Vietnam.

The cultivator class includes farmers, woodsmen, and fishermen. Since Vietnam is primarily an agriculture and fishing country, this class was the majority of the population, about 80 to 90 percent. The primary agriculture crop in Vietnam is rice. Rice cultivation is a labor-intensive process that requires both human power and animal assistance. Water buffaloes serve as the principal animal working side by side with the farmers. As such, the water buffalo has become an important cultural symbol in Vietnamese folklore and children's stories. Over the years Vietnamese artists and musicians have romanticized the simple life of a young boy tending water buffaloes in rice fields, and there is a national longing for the happiness associated with that picture.

The laborer class includes those who do manual labor as well as specialized craftspeople, such as carpenters, goldsmiths, bricklayers, potters, lacquer artists, and shoemakers. These occupations require specialized skills that are often passed on from one generation to the next. There are villages that specialize in specific crafts and provide the entire country with their finished products. Throughout the country, some villages have names that reflect the craft in which they have specialized. For example, a village might be well known for making beautiful pottery, whereas another one a few miles away is recognized for making fine furniture. In the larger cities, there are boulevards that are named for the products and specialized food that are produced and sold on those streets.

The merchant or business class in ancient Vietnam is often looked down on and is considered the undesirable class because business transactions were generally seen as a means to cheating others. Since most people worked and sold their products to earn a living, members of this class were not seen as practicing similar types of professions. Since business transactions do not result in the making of any particular product, they were generally seen as stealing the labor and products from those who made them.

The final class includes primarily soldiers. Since Vietnam has had a long history of fighting wars against foreign invaders, it has been important for this class to receive support from all the other classes in order to defend the country. Members of this class were not expected to produce any products or to be engaged in intensive labor, rather, they were expected to train as soldiers and to stand ready to defend the country in times of war. As in armies throughout the world, members of this class were primarily young men who were trained by, and answered to, an older group of military officers.

Respect

In traditional Vietnamese society, respect as a cultural value is deeply embedded in all social relations and interactions as well as in all the activities of daily life. Thus, the social hierarchy of the society is clearly observed and maintained in everyday life.

The cultural value of respect can be seen in the Vietnamese language by the proliferation of titles designating the relative position of an individual vis-à-vis another person. For example, in Vietnamese, the title designates not only the family relationship such as mother, father, aunt, uncle, sister, brother, grandmother, and grandfather but also which side of the family that individual comes from. In other words, when used, the title clearly reveals whether that person is from one's paternal or maternal side and whether it is an older or younger relative. When siblings are described, the term reveals whether the sister or brother is younger ("*em,*" for women and men) or older ("chi" for women and "anh"men, respectively). When addressing strangers, the person's title is judged in relation to one's parents. If they are seen as older than one's parents, they are generally referred to as "*bac*" (older uncle or aunt), and "*chu*" or "*co*" (younger uncle or aunt, respectively) for someone younger.

Another way in which respect is shown is by avoiding eye contact with someone who is higher in status because of their education, social standing, age, or gender. Direct eye contact generally conveys a direct challenge or an expression of intimate passion. One must also bow the head slightly in the presence of an elderly person, which also conveys respect.

Harmony

The art of peacefulness and living in harmony is more highly valued than a show of conflict. In any social interaction, open disagreement or the raising of one's voice disturbs the harmony of one's self and those around you. As a result, Vietnamese tend to seek out peaceful resolutions and avoid shaming others in public. This cultural practice is often misunderstood by non-Vietnamese since Vietnamese tend to nod in agreement with things even though they might disagree. This act of agreement is primarily carried out in order to be harmonious and to not offend the other person, and not necessarily because the person agrees. For example, a Buddhist man was asked by his U.S. sponsor to attend a Christian church service on a Sunday with him. The man could not say "No" because he did not want to be seen as ungrateful to his U.S. sponsor but chose to say "yes" instead to make the situation harmonious (Rutledge, 1992). From the Vietnamese way of thinking, his American sponsor might have understood his response later if the sponsor had reflected on the fact that it would have been inappropriate for him to attend church because he was in fact Buddhist. The Vietnamese man acted in a culturally appropriate manner to avoid embarrassing the sponsor for his lack of understanding. Without this cultural understanding, it can be frustrating for both parties involved because from an American's perspective, if one agrees to do something, one should follow through. However, from the Vietnamese's point of view, it would be the responsibility of the other person to understand their circumstances and to not request things that are unreasonable.

Cardinal Virtues

A person in the traditional Vietnamese culture is thought to be incomplete, or not virtuous, without the mastery of the following five cardinal virtues: *nhan, nghia, le, tri, tin* (benevolence or compassion; righteousness; propriety;

wisdom or learning; and truthfulness). *Nhan* refers to the nature of the human relationship between different people. A child must be filial toward the parents. A sibling should show loving care toward other siblings. A person should treat another person with respect, compassion, and love. *Nghia* implies duty, justice, and obligation. This concept reveals the expected social behaviors and interactions within the structure of the traditional society where one is expected to behave in a certain way, depending on one's social status. For example, *nghia* dictates how a younger brother should behave toward an older brother, a son to a father, or a subject to a king. It also requires one to give back what one has received either directly or indirectly from others. A person must understand that it is important to give something back because one does not and cannot achieve by one's self. For example, when one receives a doctorate, it was not simply because of the individual's own ability but also because of the support provided by the entire family. *Le* demands a person to be polite and civil to other people. This is the quality or state of being proper in a person's behavior in society. A person must act in good manners to show respect and understanding for other people. *Tri* focuses on how one uses one's intelligence to make important decisions about life. It also expresses the ability to wisely use one's intelligence and wisdom in daily life in order to create happiness. *Tin* is the concept of truthfulness. A person must be truthful in one's entire life. This is especially true with respect to promises made to family members, friends, and colleagues. A person's word has to be kept in order to build trust with other people. It demands a person to be honest in all social interactions with others, regardless of their social status in society.

CUISINE

In general, Vietnamese food is lighter than Chinese food and uses a variety of spices and fresh vegetables. Since Vietnam is an agricultural and fishing country, the main staples are rice, vegetables, and fish. While there are several varieties, rice is simply categorized in two primary ways: ordinary rice of various types that is cooked as part of the daily food or pounded into powder to make different types of noodles and the various forms of sticky rice that are generally steamed ("xoi") and often used at ritual ceremonies. Vietnamese eat rice several times a day in either small or large bowls with a lot of vegetables and little meat or fish. An important ingredient in Vietnamese cuisine is *nuoc mam* or fish sauce. This sauce is made by combining water, fish extract, and salt and marinating it in large kegs for a month. This condiment is used either with fresh lime juice, chili peppers, and garlic as a dipping sauce to help add flavor to the vegetables, or as a way to make salty dishes to help Vietnamese eat more rice. In general, Vietnamese do not eat large quantities of meat. When meat is served, it is generally cut into slivers to stir fry with vegetables or in larger pieces to cook with brine. Chicken and eggs supplement this diet. All of these ingredients are typically available fresh at the market each morning. Vietnamese generally go to the local food market on a daily basis. An additional dietary food, introduced as a result of the long French occupation, is bread. The rice diet is supplemented with bread, which has become widely consumed by all Vietnamese.

One of Vietnam's favorite dishes is a noodle soup called *pho*. The dish itself originated from North Vietnam, but it is generally eaten by everyone. It is made with chicken or beef broth prepared with a variety of spices. The broth is poured into a bowl with cooked rice noodles and thin slices of beef or chicken that are either rare or cooked, and finally scallions and cilantro are added on top. *Pho* is normally accompanied at the table with a plate of lime slices, bean sprouts, and sweet basil along with some chili sauce and hoisan sauce (a brown sauce made of sugar, vinegar, soya bean, water and salt) added for taste. Although traditionally a morning meal in Vietnam, *pho* is now served anytime in noodle shops in the United States.

BRIEF HISTORY

The history of Vietnam dates back more than four thousand years. Therefore, the history presented here will necessarily be incomplete and will focus primarily on the last 350 years with an emphasis on the influence of China, the French occupation, and the United States' involvement in Vietnam and the Vietnam War.

According to mythical legends, Vietnamese are the offspring produced by the marriage of a dragon and a fairy. The marriage, of the Dragon Lord of the Lac and the mountain princess of fairy blood named Au Co, produced one hundred children. Since a dragon and a fairy could not live together, the children were divided between the parents—half of the children returned to the sea with their father and the other half settled in the Red River with their mother. One of the children became the first King of the Vietnamese people, thus begins the legend of Vietnam.

The historical origins of Vietnam began in 208 B.C. when Trieu Da, a renegade Chinese General, conquered Au Lac, a province in the northern mountains of Vietnam, established a capitol city, and declared himself emperor of "Nam Viet." Since that period, the history of Vietnam has been one of rebellion against Chinese domination and influence. In the first century

B.C., the Han dynasty of China expanded and incorporated Nam Viet into the Chinese Empire as the province of Giao Chi. Many rebellions followed, among which the most famous is that of the Trung sisters' (Trung Nhi and Trung Trach) insurrection against the Chinese in 40 A.D. After the Chinese executed a high-ranking Vietnamese lord, his widow and her sister organized and lead a rebellion against the Chinese. The two sisters defeated a more powerful Chinese army and declared themselves queens of the newly independent Vietnam. Unfortunately, three years later, the Chinese attacked and defeated the Vietnamese. Rather than surrender, the two Trung sisters, committed suicide by jumping into the Hat Giang River. This event immortalized them and served as the impetus to set up an independent state. In 967, Emperor Dinh Bo Linh ascended his throne, calling his new state Dai Co Viet. A period of independence followed before the next wave of foreign invasion.

Chinese Occupation

From its beginning, the history of Vietnam has been turbulent. Foreign domination and influence have been continuous. One of the most outstanding historical characteristics of Vietnam has been its seemingly unending fight against foreign domination. Among the countries that have had a history of foreign occupation in Vietnam are China, France, Japan, and the United States. Each of these countries left a legacy and an influence in the political, social, cultural, and historical development of Vietnam.

Vietnam has been greatly influenced by China. In fact, a popular Vietnamese folk song reminds Vietnamese of their history and that there has been "one thousand years of the Chinese domination, one hundred years of the domination by the French, and twenty years of internal Civil War fighting." In many ways, this folk song represents a short and overall history of Vietnam. In 1428, after a decade of revolt led by Emperor Le Loi, the Chinese recognized Vietnam's independence and signed an accord. Emperor Le Loi's dynasty lasted three centuries. From 1460 to 1498, Le Thanh Tong ruled Vietnam and introduced a comprehensive legal code and other reforms. During this period Vietnam extended its territory southward by conquering the kingdoms of Champa and Cambodia, its neighbors to the south.

Despite China's continuous attempt to conquer Vietnam and make it part of China, Vietnam developed a very distinct set of cultural values and practices. Because there are too many cultural characteristics to list, a few important examples will suffice to illustrate this point. The first distinct cultural difference is the practice of chewing betel (*an trau*). The Vietnamese proverb,

"*Mieng trau la dau cau chuyen*," or "Eating of the betel is the beginning of the story," illustrates the importance of this social and cultural tradition. The practice of chewing betel is thought to have begun during the Van Lang period. The Van Lang Kingdom began in the seventh century B.C. and is an important historical and cultural past for the Vietnamese. Betel is a plant that is chewed primarily by Vietnamese women and a smaller number of men as a stimulant. Betel chewing is generally combined with a bitter dried fruit, a small pinch of tobacco, and a mixture of lime (generally dyed pink or red). This cultural practice is deeply embedded in many celebrations and is presented as a part of required gifts during important social and cultural events, including engagement parties, wedding ceremonies, and funerals. Although chewing betel is no longer readily practiced in cities, many women continue to chew betel as a part of their daily life in the countryside.

The second distinct culture difference is the practice of blackening one's teeth. Although thought to be the result of chewing betel, the practice of blackening one's teeth has its own cultural and social significance. Traditionally, this process would not take place until the person's permanent teeth are in place. The process requires a series of chemical treatments in order to achieve the final goal of having one's teeth completely black. The darker the teeth, the more attractive the individual. Although the practice of blackening one's teeth declined after 1945, a number of older Vietnamese has blackened teeth and some people living in rural villages still follow the practice.

The third cultural difference is reflected in the ways in which Vietnamese women and men dress. The unmistakable Vietnamese "*ao dai*," or long dress, is quite different and distinct from Chinese dresses. The *ao dai* is the national dress of Vietnam, one that is worn by men and women at all important and significant social, cultural, and familial events. Although the influences of France and the United States have contributed to some changes in the ways in which people dress in their daily lives, the *ao dai* remains the national dress for women, as well as the constant symbol of how Vietnamese distinguish themselves from their neighbors.

Although successful at resisting total assimilation by the Chinese, the Vietnamese did not emerge from Chinese rule unchanged. China succeeded in influencing Vietnamese institutions including law, administration, education, literature, language, and culture. The greatest class to be impacted was the Vietnamese elite, with whom China had the most contact. The least influenced were the common people, with whom China had little contact. The Chinese occupation as well as the Vietnamese resistance and rebellion continued throughout Vietnamese history until the next foreign domination, that of France.

French Occupation

The French officially entered Vietnam in 1777, a time when other European powers, such as Great Britain, Spain, and the Netherlands, were colonizing other countries around the world. The French influence began in Vietnam as early as 1627 when Alexandre de Rhodes, a French missionary, changed the Vietnamese language (*Chu Nom*) from Chinese characters to the roman alphabet (*Chu Quoc Ngu*). However, it was in 1777, under the pretense of assisting a peasant rebellion uprising against the ruling Vietnamese families, that France exerted its military power. After the defeat of Vietnam by a superior French military power, the Treaty of 1787 gave France exclusive trading rights and access to the ports in Vietnam. In the early period, the initial influence was primarily cultural and religious. In fact, in 1787, Monsignor Pierre Joseph Georges Pigneau de Behaine, Bishop of Adran, wanted to create a Christian empire in Asia under the auspices of and with France's blessing. However, the terms of this treaty were interrupted by the French Revolution in 1789 and the Napoleonic wars that followed.

As a result of domestic events, France attempted to renegotiate the terms of the 1787 treaty with Vietnam but met with little success. Although unsuccessful in their political negotiations, French Catholic missionaries succeeded at converting a sizable number of Vietnamese to Catholicism. Beginning in the 1820s, fearing the effects and influence of a growing Vietnamese Catholic minority by the French missionaries, different Vietnamese Emperors began to outlaw and persecute missionaries and their converts. The French government quickly used this act of religious persecution to land its troops in an attempt to once again exert its political influence and military power in Vietnam. When in 1858 two priests—one French and one Spanish—were killed, a joint Franco-Spanish expedition was organized to save other missionaries. Even though Spain stopped after the Vietnamese government gave assurances of non-persecution in the future, the French continued the war for three years until France finally signed a treaty with Emperor Tu Duc in 1862. After a series of battles, conflicts, legal maneuvers, and treaties, France finally succeeded in defeating Vietnam militarily and politically, although it was not until the 1890s that France gained complete control of Vietnam.

As soon as they were able to establish military and political control in the country, the French colonial government implemented a policy of iron-fist political control and economic exploitation. The country was divided into three administrative areas; Tonkin, Annam, and Cochinchina—roughly corresponding to the areas referred to by Vietnamese as Bac Bo (northern Vietnam), Trung Bo (central Vietnam), and Nam Bo (southern Vietnam). There emerged a small elite, mostly French-educated, ruling Vietnamese class and a large and growing number of poor and impoverished peasants who were dislocated from their villages and farms. The French ruling elite also introduced rubber plantations in the south, over 90 percent of which were French owned. In addition, the French had a monopoly on salt, alcohol, and opium. As was true in other Asian countries at the time, the Vietnamese economy and the production process became one geared for foreign exportation and not for domestic consumption. Vietnamese were denied many basic rights such as the freedom of speech, access to jobs, land ownership, and participation in the political process. This pattern of colonization is similar to that of other Asian countries during this time period where colonies were established by European countries.

As a result of French rule, which was politically repressive and economically exploitative, there were continuous arms rebellions throughout the country. Vietnamese-organized resistance movements in the early years were led by members of the scholar and official class, many of whom refused to cooperate with the French government by relinquishing their official positions in protest. Different philosophical views concerning resistance toward the French generally fell into two schools of thought. One view argued that the return of the monarchy would serve as a focal point around which to organize and rally people. It was felt that if power were restored to the monarchy, the people would support a struggle for independence. The other school advocated using Western democratic ideas as a way to struggle against the French. They believed that if the principles of democracy, freedom, and rights were introduced to the masses, the people would rise up and struggle for national independence. Regardless of their differences in philosophy, members of both schools of thought were all nationalists whose primary goal was to defeat the French government in Vietnam and to achieve independence for Vietnam.

Most of these rebellions—such as those led by Phan Dinh Phung, Hoang Hoa Tham, Phan Boi Chau, Phan Chau Trinh, and Nguyen Thai Hoc—were rurally based guerrilla resistance movements. The leaders of these rebellions were educated individuals who wanted independence for Vietnam. The most significant of these rebellions was the Revolutionary Youth Movement in 1925 by Nguyen Thai Hoc, who changed his name in 1943 to Ho Chi Minh. This organization evolved into the Indochina Communist Party in 1929, which became the Vietnamese Communist Party in 1930. All nationalist movements were ruthlessly and successfully repressed by the French government in Vietnam. As a result, many of the resistance leaders were put to death, forced underground, or exiled.

Japanese Occupation

During World War II, when France fell to Germany in June of 1940, Marshal Philippe Petain was forced to set up a puppet French government in Vichy. As a result of a general accord signed between France and Japan in September 1940, and despite the fact that Vietnam was now under the control of Japan, the French colonial administration was left intact by the Japanese government. In effect, Asian imperialism had been substituted for European imperialism in Vietnam. Vietnamese nationalists continued to rebel against both the French and the Japanese, and they continued to rally and advocate for Vietnam's independence.

With the defeat of Japan by the United States in 1945, a vacuum of power was created, and it was temporarily filled by Ho Chi Minh and his followers. Under the ruling of Japan, Ho Chi Minh and his followers were able to receive some public support as a result of their successes in using guerrilla warfare to undermine the more powerful Japanese and French military. Shortly thereafter, the French, with support from Great Britain and the United States, invaded Vietnam in an attempt to reassert their colonial control. After nine years of armed struggles, the French were soundly defeated by the Viet Minh at the battle of Dien Bien Phu in May 1954. This led to the Geneva Conference in 1954 to determine a provisional demarcation line at the 17th parallel dividing Vietnam into two separate regions, pending a political settlement after a nationwide election to be held in 1956.

According to the Geneva Accord, the national election scheduled for 1956 was to provide Vietnam with a unified and independent country. However, realizing that Ho Chi Minh, a communist, could win the national election, the United States gave its support to Ngo Dinh Diem, a little-known and unpopular Catholic leader. Diem proposed the creation of an independent Republic of South Vietnam with himself as the Prime Minister. As a result of widespread rumors of a possible bloodbath if the Vietnamese Catholics stayed in the North, almost a million people left northern Vietnam in 1954, two thirds of whom were Catholic. The end result of this political maneuvering was that the country was in effect divided in two, with Ngo Dinh Diem as prime minister in the newly formed Republic of Vietnam in the South and Ho Chi Minh as president of the Democratic Vietnam in the North.

These historical events marked a critical period immediately before the beginning of the escalation of the United States's direct involvement in Vietnam.

THE UNITED STATES AND VIETNAM: A BRIEF HISTORY

World War II

For the United States, World War II, and to a lesser extent the Cold War, had encouraged feelings of unity and a sense of national purpose and had generated pressures for domestic accommodation. The war in Vietnam produced the very opposite: fragmentation, alienation, confrontation, and what the editors of *Time* magazine would call "the loss of a working consensus, for the first time in our lives, as to what we think American means" (Polenberg, 1980). The Vietnam War deeply divided people in the United States.

The United States first entered the Vietnamese conflict when President Truman's administration (1945–1949) provided foreign aid to the French. This foreign aid grew quite rapidly from "approximately $150 million per year in 1950 to over $1 billion in the fiscal year of 1954," when the United States was underwriting 80 percent of the cost of the war. This escalation can be seen both in terms of military support and in financial aid. For example, by the end of the Eisenhower administration (January 1961) there were 600 American advisors in Vietnam. When President John F. Kennedy was assassinated in November 1963, more than 16,000 American soldiers were in Vietnam, most of whom were beyond the advising stage. Under President Lyndon B. Johnson's administration, the number of American advisors stood at 25,000 on January 1, 1965. By 1966 this number escalated to 184,000 and to 385,000 by 1967. President Richard M. Nixon followed this policy and the number of American soldiers continued to rise to 485,000 by 1968 and to 536,000 by 1969 (Polenberg, 1980).

Escalation and U.S. Policies

The decision to intervene in Vietnam derived from assumptions President Johnson shared with Secretary of State Dean Rusk, Secretary of Defense Robert McNamara, Special Assistant for National Security Affairs McGeorge Bundy, and nearly all his other advisers. These assumptions were rooted in a conviction that the events in Southeast Asia in the 1960s paralleled those of Europe in the 1940s that gave rise to communism which then took a strong hold throughout Eastern Europe. The conflict in Vietnam, they believed, was the result of the attack of North Vietnam on South Vietnam and a definite act of communist aggression. Therefore, if the United States did not intervene, communism would spread throughout Asia, and other Asian countries would begin to tumble, one after the other. This theory is generally referred to as the "domino theory."

However, while President Johnson's administration denied publicly any intention of intervening in Vietnam, it had a desire to do so. This road to war took three steps. First, President Johnson announced the Gulf of Tonkin incident where North Vietnamese boats were alleged to have attacked and fired at an American destroyer in international waters on August 1, 1964. Three days later, the USS Maddox alleged a second attack by North Vietnam. These events were portrayed as clear acts of aggression against the United States by the North Vietnamese. On August 4, 1964, President Johnson announced to the American public that he had ordered retaliatory military measures. At the same time, he was also seeking support from Congress by introducing the Gulf of Tonkin Resolution to Congress. After the overwhelming passage of the Tonkin Resolution by Congress, President Johnson received authorization from Congress "as Commander in Chief, to take all necessary measures to repel any armed attack against the forces of the United States and to prevent further aggression" (McMahon, 1995).

The second step taken by President Johnson was the bombardment of North Vietnam in the fall of 1964 after nine "military advisors" were killed and more than one hundred Americans were wounded in Pleiku, a city in Central Vietnam. The third and final step was the decision to send American ground troops into Vietnam. The escalation of fighting, the increase of military troops sent to Vietnam, and the financing of the conflict continued until the Tet Mau Than (New Year) Offensive of 1968. Prior to this event, the administration and General Westmoreland had successfully convinced the American public that the United States was winning the war or that, at least, there was a light at the end of the tunnel and that the troops would be coming home soon.

The Tet Mau Than Offensive of 1968 jolted the American public. Tet, the lunar New Year celebration, is one of the most important cultural celebrations in Vietnam. Prior to this military event, most of the American media coverage reported only routine activities of the war in Vietnam, including American soldiers on patrols, regular bombing of different communist installations, questioning of captured prisoners, and standard military operations. The then commonly held belief reported by the government was that the American troops and the South Vietnamese government had complete control of the country. However, during that brief period, the Viet Cong (South Vietnamese communists), who deliberately violated their agreement for a cease fire during the holidays, were able to launch an all-out offensive attack and successfully capture many important military installations. They were also able to penetrate the capital city of Saigon and briefly capture the U.S. Embassy. The capture of the U.S. Embassy in Saigon stunned and shocked the American public who believed that the U.S. Embassy was impenetrable. During this period, the U.S. media concentrated on more specific events and covered war activities in much greater depth, giving more detail, including footage of numerous violent, bloody, and explicit scenes from the battlefields. One example of a horrific scene that became famous and that was shown nationally on the networks' nightly news was that of Nguyen Ngoc Loan, the Saigon police chief, shooting a captured enemy, presumably a Viet Cong, in the head point blank. The picture was extremely explicit and violent. This picture and others like it created intense debate and raised objections from television viewers throughout the country. What was unknown and not revealed to the U.S. public at that time was the fact that the prisoner had just killed a number of soldiers and civilians, including women and children. Nevertheless, these explicit pictures from the Vietnam War, and the Tet Offensive in particular, left an indelible impression on the hearts and minds of the American public. In the end, although thoroughly defeated at the time, the Viet Cong succeeded in their primary mission and ultimate goal: to turn U.S. public sentiment against the continuation of military and financial support for the Vietnam War. For General Vo Nguyen Giap, the commander in chief of the North Vietnamese troops, this was a great tactical victory. Although very costly in terms of the number of communist soldiers killed during the Tet Offensive, this victory was to be the beginning of the end of the Vietnam War. As the war went on, General Giap realized that there was very little chance that the Vietnamese communist army could defeat the more powerful and technologically more advanced U.S. military. However, if he could somehow cause the American public to stop supporting the war, that, in effect, the war would be won. The primary goal of General Giap during the Tet Offensive was not military victory, but rather to bring the war to an end by winning his appeal to American public opinion.

At the same time these events were taking place in Vietnam, there was a growing number of anti-war protests staged by students and others all over the United States. Media coverage of the war and these mass demonstrations brought the war home to the American public. Nightly news coverage brought war images into millions of American homes. These images were constantly bombarding the American public, and questions began to be raised about the role of the United States in the war. For the first time, major elements of U.S. society, including business leaders, the press, churches, professional groups, clergy, college and university faculty, Vietnam veterans, students, and most of the intellectual community had turned against the Vietnam War. As a result of increasing public opposition to the war and the strong urging of his advisors, President Johnson finally agreed to stop sending troops and to discontinue military escalation. He also withdrew personally and did not accept the nomination of his party for another term as President.

Despite these events, the Vietnam War did not end with President Johnson's unexpected refusal of his nomination for another term as President on March 31, 1968, nor did it end with the inauguration of the next president of the United States, Richard M. Nixon. While President Nixon was fulfilling his presidential campaign promise to withdraw troops from Vietnam—from 467,000 in 1970 to 335,000 in 1971, to 157,000 in 1972, and finally 24,000 in 1973—he simultaneously carried out secret plans to continue to bomb Vietnam, Cambodia, and Laos. In January 1973, after numerous negotiations with North Vietnam, the United States finally agreed to a cease fire and to withdraw its remaining troops.

The Vietnam War finally came to an end on April 30, 1975.

NOTES

1. Although this is the way Vietnamese spell Viet Nam, in the rest of the book I will use the more commonly accepted way Americans spell "Vietnam."

2. See Chapter 2 for a more in-depth description of the mass exodus of ethnic Chinese from Vietnam.

2

Vietnamese Immigration History

HISTORICAL OVERVIEW

On January 28, 1973, after having spent years and millions of dollars financing the Vietnam War, the U.S. government agreed to withdraw its financial and military assistance after signing the Agreement on Ending the War and Restoring Peace in Vietnam. The peace agreement was signed by representatives of the U.S. government, the Government of the Republic of Vietnam (South Vietnam), and the Government of the Democratic Republic of Vietnam (North Vietnam) in Paris. The main features of the Agreement committed the United States and other signatories to respect the independence, sovereignty, unity, and territorial integrity of Vietnam. It called for prisoners of war to be exchanged, and declared an in-place cease fire. The agreement also required the United States to "stop all its military activities against the territory of the Democratic Republic of Vietnam by ground, air, and naval forces wherever they may be based; and end the mining of the territorial waters, ports, harbors, and waterways of the Democratic Republic of Vietnam." Furthermore, it required the United States to "not continue its military involvement or intervene in the internal affairs of South Vietnam." This agreement was enthusiastically approved by the North Vietnamese and signed by the United States and South Vietnam's President Thieu.

However, soon after the withdrawal of U.S. military and economic support, the military situation deteriorated rapidly for the government of South Vietnam. The flight of the Vietnamese refugees began within the country, with the North Vietnamese military offensive of mid-March 1975 resulting in the defeats at Pleiku, Kontum, and Ban Me Thuot. As a result of this military offensive, about one million refugees poured out of these areas and headed for the capital city, Saigon, and the coast. Most traveled by foot; a few were fortunate enough to travel by car, truck, or motorbike. The coastal city of Da Nang was evacuated on 27 and 28 of March 1975. This was soon followed by the evacuation of other coastal cities, such as Nha Trang and Cam Ranh. President Thieu resigned on April 21, 1975, and was succeeded by Vice Prime Minister Huong. As political, economic, and military conditions continued to deteriorate even further, Vice Prime Minister Huong transferred the remaining government power to General "Big" Minh. By the end of April 1975, South Vietnam, under the direction of General Minh, surrendered to the North Vietnamese Communist government. On April 30, 1975, Saigon, the capital of South Vietnam and, thus, all of South Vietnam, came under the control of the Provisional Revolutionary Government. This resulted in the plight which brought the newest Asian Pacific immigrant group to the United States.

THE VIETNAMESE REFUGEE IMMIGRATION EXPERIENCE

Vietnamese emigration is generally divided into two periods, each with several "waves." The first period began in April 1975 and continued through 1977. This period included the first three waves of Vietnamese refugees in the United States.

The first wave of refugees, involving some ten to fifteen thousand people, began at least a week to ten days before the collapse of the government. The second wave, and probably the largest in numbers, involved some eighty thousand who were evacuated by aircraft during the last days of April. The evacuation of American personnel, their dependents, and Vietnamese affiliated with them was achieved through giant helicopters under "Operation Frequent Wind." According to *Newsweek* magazine (May 12, 1975), it was a "logistical success . . . the biggest helicopter lift of its kind in history."

These new immigrants were relatively well educated, spoke some English, had some marketable skills, came from urban areas, and were Westernized. Members of these two waves were primarily Vietnamese who worked for the U.S. government, businesses, and corporations, or the Vietnamese government. All were thought to be prepared for life in the United States on the basis of their contact with the U.S. government and association with Americans.

Quyen, a 23-year-old female college student majoring in business economics recalls her experience leaving Vietnam:

We came to the United States in 1975. My dad was an officer in the navy. We were going to stay outside on the ocean until the war was over and come back in because they did not think we were going to lose. But it turned out that we lost and so we kept going and going out until we saw this big old boat. . . . The boat that picked us up was an American cargo ship. They took us to an island and after what seemed like forever, we were taken to Guam Island.

The final wave during this period involved forty to sixty thousand people who left on their own in small boats, ships, and commandeered aircraft during the first two weeks of May 1975. They were later transferred to Subic Bay and Clark Air Force base in the Philippines and Guam Island after having been picked up, in many cases, by the U.S. Navy and cargo ships standing off the coast of Vietnam. Kim-Phuong, a graduating senior at the University of California, Santa Barbara, majoring in biological sciences recalls her family's narrow escape from Vietnam:

We came during the summer. I remember my mom telling us to pack all our stuff and we were supposed to meet our father at the beach outside of Saigon. Our dad . . . had access to a boat so he met us there. I was only five but I remember it took a long time to get to where we wanted to go. I think we walked for a day. . . . I just remember rushing and rushing. . . . We got on a boat and we just went out to the water, we didn't know where we were going, we were just going out toward the ocean. We were finally picked up by an American ship.

The second period of the Vietnamese refugees migration began in 1978 and continues even today. Since the fall of South Vietnam in 1975, many Vietnamese have tried to escape the political oppression, the major social, political, and economic reforms instituted by the authoritarian communist government of North Vietnam. Although the influx continues steadily, the numbers are no longer as massive as they once were. A significant characteristic of this period, especially between the years 1978 to 1980, was the large number of ethnic Chinese who migrated out of Vietnam and Cambodia. The following is an account of this migration process by Phu, a college sophomore ethnic Chinese majoring in biological sciences:

I don't know how much it cost us but we had to do a lot of paper work. We had to go through the communist government. Since paper money was unacceptable, the way we had to pay the fees was in gold.

You had to be Chinese, or of Chinese descent or something like that in order to go. . . . Our goal was to go to Hong Kong but it ended up that our captain did not know the way. We met and stopped two fishermen in the middle of the ocean and had to do some business with them before they would show us the way to Hong Kong. In the end, they didn't really show us the way, they just pointed and told us to go straight. We were somehow lucky enough to finally get to Hong Kong.

In addition to the Vietnamese ethnic Chinese, many Vietnamese also left during this period. These individuals have been called "Vietnamese boat people" because most of them escaped in homemade, poorly constructed boats and wooden vessels. Due to the lack of sophistication of their vessels, which could not withstand the forces of nature, their scant knowledge of navigational skills, the limited amount of provisions they were able to bring, and, finally, numerous attacks by Thai sea pirates, the death rate of the "Vietnamese boat people" was very high. Some verbal testimony from surviving refugees in many refugee camps estimates the number to be as high as 50 percent, while Grant (1979) and Wain (1981) have placed it at 10 percent to 15 percent. However, the percentage will never be accurately known since there is no systematic way of knowing how many refugees actually left Vietnam, and only survivors are accounted for. Because of the chaotic nature of the war and the secrecy employed by those who left Vietnam, the Vietnamese communist government did not keep track of emigrés. Since 1979, many former receiving countries have turned away refugees because of the economic, political, and social strain that they put on their economies. The following accounts are from two individuals who left Vietnam five years apart. The first account is from a refugee who arrived in 1981. She was lucky, her entire family was able to leave together.

After 1975, my mom and dad had a small mom-and-pop shop where the whole family worked together. We all worked there. . . . The journey lasted ten days and we went straight to Thailand. The boat was pretty small, only about sixteen meters long and there were thirty-six people cramped in it. We were fortunate, there were few problems during our journey. We came to Thailand and lived there for three years and went to Indonesia. We finally came to the United States later.

The second account is from Huynh. He was not as fortunate, having left Vietnam by himself in 1985, leaving behind his parents and his other siblings:

Our lives before 1975 were pretty normal. Both of my parents were into business and so they had a small shop selling everything. Once the communists came in, we were restricted a lot more in terms of our business activities. In fact, we tried to escape in 1975 but were caught at Phu Quoc [an island off the southern coast] and all of us spent two months in prison. Afterward, when we came out, we were left with nothing. They took our small shop. . . . My father was then sent to re-education camp for nine years. My mother was left behind to take care of the eight of us. In 1978, when my older brothers were threatened to be drafted into the military, my uncle (who lived in the United States at the time) sent money for their journey out of Vietnam. They both left in 1978. I finally left in 1985. . . . The journey was long and often times frightening. I didn't know where we were going but we ended in Indonesia.

In sum, the exodus of Vietnamese refugees to the United States was a difficult process. Regardless of which period they came from, the journey to America left a lasting impression on all those involved. For some, the long journey was made easier because they were able to leave during the earlier period when restrictions were not as severe, or when they were younger. For others, the journey was more traumatic because of their family circumstances, or because they had been caught previously trying to escape and were sent to prison. Despite the differences, the uncertain and dangerous journey across the vast ocean to a new and unknown destination made it a difficult journey for all.

U.S. RESPONSE

The Vietnamese exodus and their resettlement in the United States could not have come at a worse time in U.S. history. The Vietnam War was an extremely unpopular war at home: 57,692 American men and women had died and 2,500 were listed as missing in action or as prisoners of war (Capps, 1982). The war divided the nation deeply.

Indeed, the general attitude of the American public at the end of the war was one of hostility toward the Vietnamese refugees. A Gallup Poll taken in May 1975 showed "54 percent of all Americans opposed to admitting Vietnamese refugees to live in the United States and only 36 percent were in favor with 12 percent undecided" (*Time*, May 19, 1975). A common concern of the American public was one of economic self-interest—a fear of having jobs taken away as well as having too much public assistance and welfare given the refugees. During this time, the United States was in a period of recession with an unemployment rate of 8.3 percent (Kelly, 1977). In fact, on April 27, 1975, over 60,000 angry unemployed union members poured on the Robert F. Kennedy stadium in Washington, D.C., to protest the lack of employment opportunities. The May 12, 1975, issue of *Newsweek* quoted California Congressman Burt Talcott as having said, "Damn it, we have too many Orientals already. If they all gravitate to California, the tax and welfare rolls will get overburdened and we already have our share of illegal aliens." The same issue reported this statement by an Arkansas woman: "They say it is a lot colder here than in Vietnam. With a little luck, maybe all those Vietnamese will take pneumonia and die." Even liberal Democrats such as California Governor Edmund Brown and Senator George McGovern said negative things about the entire refugee operation. Several early studies documented that a substantial number of Americans preferred the exclusion of the refugees from the United States. Apart from specific conditions resulting from the Vietnam War and the economic recession, this hostile reception given by the American public represented a continuation of racism and hostility toward immigrant minority groups that has prevailed and been well documented throughout the United States' history.

The Vietnamese refugees, therefore, arrived in the United States with a legacy of hostility directed toward Asians. Most of the hostility was racially and economically based. Despite these attitudes, many other Americans extended humanitarian aid and sponsored families from refugee camps. There were those who did not want them here because of the war, the economic competition, racism, and other factors. There were also others who felt responsible for their arrival and were motivated for humanitarian reasons.

Many refugees who escaped from Vietnam during the second period opted to make countries closest to their own their destinations. As a result, Hong Kong, Thailand, Malaysia, Indonesia, Singapore, and the Philippines all hosted refugee camps. As refugees began to arrive in these countries in large numbers, each host government began to seek support from the international community in order to provide the necessary assistance. Originally, the main purpose of these refugee camps was to control the movement of people and to channel them toward resettlement countries. Gradually, however, these camps began to serve as holding centers where refugees were processed and evaluated to determine their eligibility as asylum seekers.

Southeast Asian refugee camps shared some general characteristics. They were primarily located in areas away from the indigenous population. The degree of autonomy and freedom in each camp varied according to the country and the local authorities. Input from the refugees themselves ranged from

Unaccompanied minors with language teacher in Thai refugee camp, 1991. Photo courtesy of Akemi Flynn.

none—where conditions were prison-like—to some—where conditions were more open and refugees were allowed to support themselves by working in the local community and were allowed to travel with day passes.

Since these camps were thought to have been temporary, most structures were hastily constructed. Refugees were allocated small, limited living spaces. Often, three to four tiers of bunk beds were added to accommodate entire families. There were two systems by which food was allocated. Food was directly distributed and rationed by camp authorities, or food was prepared in communal kitchens and eaten in dining halls. In some cases, in order to supplement their diets, refugees cultivated small plots of land in order to grow their own fruits and vegetables. Wherever they were allowed, refugees worked as manual workers for the local communities. In some camps, small shops and businesses were established and run by the refugees.

A variety of activities was organized by agency workers in the camps. The activities were designed to encourage refugees to keep occupied. They included classes in language training, arts and crafts, typing, and tailoring. In some camps, vocational courses were offered. Although these activities were organized to motivate refugees, many found it difficult to acquire these skills when there was little chance for them to be resettled. Other activities, primarily those that were organized by refugees themselves, were received with more enthusiasm. These activities focused more on sports and musical activities. Among the most popular activities were lessons in guitar, photography, and painting. These activities allowed refugees to develop independent talents that helped them forget their mundane routines.

All refugee camps have since been closed. The last two countries to officially close camps were Hong Kong and Thailand. With the return of Hong Kong to China in 1997, there was tremendous pressure for Hong Kong to deal with Southeast Asian refugees before the official transfer. As a result, those refugees who had not been allowed to immigrate to a receiving country faced the choice of returning to Vietnam voluntarily in the earlier stages, or being forcefully returned to Vietnam. Although it was not faced with the same pressure from mainland China, Thailand also faced economic, political, and social pressures to solve the refugee question as quickly as possible and to turn their attention to the affairs of the country. Southeast Asian refugees who lived in the last remaining refugee camps in Thailand faced the same choice as those in Hong Kong. They either had to volunteer to return to Vietnam or be forced to return to Vietnam.

REFUGEE CAMPS IN THE UNITED STATES

When Vietnamese refugees first arrived in April 1975, the U.S. government had to organize temporary refugee camps in order to transfer refugees into American society or to find third-country sponsors as soon as possible. As a result, there were four camps that were quickly set up to handle the estimated number of arrivals. All of the camps were on military bases, since the bases were able to provide the necessary labor and space to accommodate large numbers of refugees. The first camp to open was at Camp Pendleton in California, followed by camps at Fort Chaffee in Arkansas, Eglin Air Force Base in Florida, and finally, Indiantown Gap in Pennsylvania.

Because of the suddenness of the refugees' arrival, the facilities were hastily set up as temporary shelters. For example, at Camp Pendleton, only twenty-four hours notice was given to the camp commander regarding the expected arrival of thousands of refugees. As a result, refugees were housed in large tents with ten cot beds in each tent. Families were assigned to these tents depending on the time of their arrival. As the number of refugees increased, so did the number of locations in each of the camps. There were many services provided to the refugees in these camps to prepare them for the transition to life outside. In addition to housing, other important services included food, showers and washing facilities, laundry areas, and recreational

Arrival at Camp Pendleton, California, 1975. Photo courtesy of Cecilia White and Connie White.

activities such as sports and entertainment. There were also educational centers where English was taught and learned by the majority of the refugees. As time went by, other services were also provided to make the transition smoother and to provide a degree of normalcy in camp life. These services included health and medical assistance, vocational training, a library, postal services, and religious programs offered by different Catholic and Christian churches and Buddhist temples. Despite these programs, inevitable difficulties occurred. Some of the problems were a result of the lack of coordination of efforts of the many different federal and state agencies involved in providing services. In many instances, the food was not compatible with the Vietnamese diet, there were not enough warm blankets and jackets for newcomers, and there were cultural misunderstandings on both sides. Despite these problems, the camps succeeded in providing the basic necessities of daily life while Vietnamese refugees were adjusting and waiting to be sponsored out of camps.

U.S. GOVERNMENT DISPERSAL POLICY

To minimize the social impact of the large influx of Vietnamese refugees on an American public that did not favor the Vietnam War, the U.S. federal

Waiting in line for food at Camp Pendleton, California, 1975. Photo courtesy of Cecilia White and Connie White.

government, under the leadership of President Gerald Ford, adapted the Refugee Dispersion Policy. The administration arrived at the policy after President Ford consulted a number of people around the country. In order for the policy to be accepted, President Ford personally lobbied members of Congress, members of his own cabinet, and other prominent community leaders around the country. The Refugee Dispersion Policy served four purposes: to relocate the Vietnamese refugees as quickly as possible so that they could achieve financial independence; to ease the impact of a large group of refugees on a given community to avoid an increase in competition for jobs; to make it logistically easier to find sponsors; and to prevent the development of an ethnic ghetto. Given the political and social climate of the United States at the time, the influential factors leading to this Dispersion Policy were primarily political and financial, not social. It was felt that if this policy was carried out successfully, the Vietnamese refugees would quickly assimilate into American society.

Nine voluntary agencies (VOLAGS) were contracted by the government's Interagency Task Force to handle the resettlement of the refugees in the United States. The agencies included the United Hebrew Immigration and Assistance Service, the Lutheran Immigration and Refugee Service, the In-

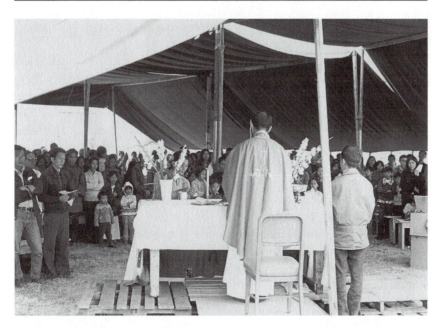

Makeshift church and service at Camp Pendleton, California, 1975. Photo courtesy of Cecilia White and Connie White.

ternational Rescue Committee, Church World Service, the American Funds for Czechoslovak Refugees, the United States Catholic Conference, the Travelers Aid International Social Service, and the Council for Nationalities Service. While in refugee camps, each family was asked to choose a resettlement agency. If the family did not have a preference, one was assigned.

The primary task of these voluntary agencies was to find sponsors that would have the ability to fulfill both financial and moral responsibilities and to match them with each refugee's families or individuals. The responsibilities of the sponsors included providing temporary food, clothing and shelter, assistance in finding employment or job training for the head of the household, enrolling the children in school, and, finally, providing ordinary medical care. In other words, the sponsors would serve as a resource to introduce the Vietnamese refugees into the American society while they were becoming economically self-supporting.

RESETTLEMENT OF VIETNAMESE REFUGEES

There were four ways for the refugees to leave the four temporary refugee camps and enter into U.S. society: resettlement to a third country, repatriation to Vietnam, proof of financial independence, and location of a sponsor through the voluntary agencies.

Although third-country resettlement was encouraged by the United States government, this avenue was rarely chosen by the Vietnamese refugees. Very few other countries offered their assistance to resettle Vietnamese refugees unless they were certified professionals in needed technical areas, had immediate relatives in that country, or could speak that country's language. These requirements were designed to discourage an influx of refugees to these countries, for it was clearly difficult for many refugees to fulfill even one of these requirements.

Only a small number of refugees chose to return to Vietnam. Darrel Montero, an anthropologist, reported that "by October 1975, repatriation had been granted to 1,546 refugees by the new government of Vietnam" (Montero, 1979). Most were military men who were forced to leave their families behind at the time of their evacuation. During the chaotic final days of the war, many people were separated from their families and the whereabouts of their family members were unknown for a while. However, once some people realized that they had left their families behind, even after a very short period of time, they chose to return to Vietnam in order to be with them. Although the desire for freedom and the fear of communism were important criteria, being with their families was a much stronger bond, and many felt compelled to return to Vietnam despite the consequences that might have been waiting for them upon their return.

The third method by which the Vietnamese refugees were allowed to leave the camps was to demonstrate financial independence. A refugee family was required by the Task Force to show proof of cash reserves totaling at least $4,000 for each member.[1] However, due to their abrupt flight from Vietnam, very few refugees could use this option. It would have been unlikely for them to have been able to obtain such a large sum of money, given the abrupt ending the war. In addition, it was unlikely that many refugees would report to the authorities their financial holdings for fear of the unknown that awaited them in this new country. They had recently lost everything and were about to start from scratch. Indeed, if they were fortunate enough to have had some money or gold, it would have been wise for them to guard it in order to have a small safety net. Consequently, the first waves of Vietnamese refugees entered U.S. society primarily through the family sponsorship method.

The sponsors found by voluntary agencies consisted of congregations, parishes or affiliates, churches, individual families, corporations, small businesses, and American companies with former Vietnamese employees. In addition, if any of the refugees had relatives already living in the United States who could fulfill the same requirements (food, clothing, shelter, school enrollment, and medical care), they could qualify as sponsors as well. However, there were only 15,000 Vietnamese living in the United States before 1975. Most of these individuals were foreign exchange students on temporary visas or wives of U.S. soldiers who had served in Vietnam. In essence, there was not an already established Vietnamese American community in the United States and, therefore, this method hardly applied to the first waves of refugees.

The family sponsorship method was later used more frequently, however, by first-wave refugees who sponsored family members and relatives stranded in Vietnam after 1975. This method was used through the implementation of two federal government–sponsored programs resulting from the Conference on Indochinese Refugees held in Geneva, Switzerland, on June 14, 1980: the Orderly Departure Program and the Humanitarian Operation program.

The goal of these programs was to "provide Vietnamese a 'viable alternative' to dangerous clandestine departure by boat or over land" (Congressional Hearing). However, this viable alternative was not as successful as anticipated as many Vietnamese refugees continued to leave by boat out of desperation and in fear of persecution from the communist government. Under the Orderly Departure and Humanitarian Operation programs, there are three categories under which Vietnamese Americans with U.S. citizenship can participate in these programs: category I—family reunification, category II—former U.S. government or firm or organization employees, etc., and category III—reeducation center detainees. As a result of these avenues, many Vietnamese families who arrived during the first and second period, who now have citizenship or, at least, permanent residence status, are using the first category to bring any remaining family members to the United States. Hoai, a college junior majoring in biological sciences reports:

> My family has been trying to bring my mother's older sister over for a couple of years now. It has taken a lot of time and a lot of money because we have to bribe many of the government agencies and numerous officials in Vietnam in order for them to speed up the process and give her family the required papers. We have been waiting for the papers to clear for at least nine months. They have told us a few times that they were on the next flight out of Saigon but they have been telling us that for a few months. . . . I think we will probably receive two weeks' notice before they will arrive. It is pretty hard on our family

economically and emotionally for all our family, but especially my mom.

As a result of the U.S. Federal Government Dispersion Policy, Vietnamese refugees were dispersed throughout the United States shortly upon arrival. Although successful at quickly dispersing Vietnamese refugees to all fifty states, the federal and state governments were in conflict with respect to the long-term cost of providing for these refugees. That is, after the initial reimbursement from the federal government, who would pay for the cost of providing bilingual education for the children? Who would pay for the cost of implementing vocational training programs? Although these questions were not clearly answered, the federal government was able to reimburse and offer some additional fundings for state governments to provide some of the services.

However, as far as Vietnamese refugees were concerned, as time went by and new government policies were implemented, other avenues have been used to immigrate to the United States. The next section examines the adaptation processes of Vietnamese immigrants to the existing structural conditions since their arrival.

THE VIETNAMESE ADAPTATION PROCESS

How did structural conditions affect the overall adaptation experience of the first Vietnamese refugees?

First, as a result of the Federal Government Refugee Dispersion Policy, Vietnamese refugees were resettled throughout the United States. Table 2.1 illustrates the results of this policy for the first waves of Vietnamese in the United States. The federal government succeeded in its stated goal to resettle Vietnamese refugees in all fifty states. With the desired outcome coming as a result of the initial resettlement of the first group, the federal government continued the Dispersion Policy throughout succeeding waves of Vietnamese refugees. Table 2.2 represents the number of Vietnamese refugees admitted to the United States between 1975 and 1982, along with the state to which they immigrated.

Second, the extended family network that existed in Vietnam was temporarily disrupted by the immigration process to the United States. In order to find churches, social organizations, small businesses, firms, families, and individuals willing to sponsor the Vietnamese refugees, many Vietnamese extended families were broken up. Only immediate family members were allowed to stay together as a family unit to be sponsored. Single people,

Table 2.1
Number of Immigrants Resettled by State as of December 31, 1975

State	Total	%	State	Total	%
Alabama	1,262	0.97	Nebraska	1,211	0.09
Alaska	81	0.06	Nevada	338	0.26
Arkansas	2,042	1.57	New Hampshire	161	0.12
Arizona	1,059	0.82	New Jersey	1,515	1.15
California	27,199	20.10	New York	3,806	2.93
Colorado	1,790	1.38	North Carolina	1,261	0.97
Connecticut	1,175	0.91	North Dakota	448	0.35
Delaware	155	0.12	Ohio	2,924	2.25
District of Columbia	1,254	0.97	Oklahoma	3,689	2.84
Florida	5,322	4.10	Oregon	2,063	1.59
Georgia	1,331	1.03	Pennsylvania	7,159	5.52
Hawaii	2,039	1.57	Rhose Island	223	0.17
Idaho	412	0.32	South Carolina	759	0.59
Illinois	3,696	2.85	South Dakota	545	0.42
Indiana	1,785	1.38	Tennessee	922	0.71
Iowa	2,593	2.00	Texas	9,130	7.03
Kansas	1,897	1.46	Utah	559	0.43
Kentucky	967	0.75	Vermont	150	0.12
Louisiana	3,602	2.76	Virginia	3,733	2.88
Maine	375	0.29	Washington	4,182	3.22
Maryland	2,319	1.79	West Vurgubua	1,821	4.40
Massachusetts	1,169	0.90	Wisconsin	195	0.15
Michigan	2,200	1.70	Wyoming	115	0.09
Minnesota	3,802	2.93	Guam	778	0.60
Mississippi	488	0.38	American Samoa	1	0.00
Missouri	2,669	2.06	Puerto Rico	1	0.00
Montana	198	0.15	Unknown	8,182	6.30
			Total	129,792	100%

Source: Kelly, 1977, Table 6, p. 154.

grandparents, and other family members who were not immediate family members were separated into small units. Despite the chaotic and abrupt nature of the Vietnamese refugees' departure, a substantial number of people came in family groups, accounting for approximately 62 percent of all the immigrants from the first two waves (Kelly, 1977). The result of the breaking

Table 2.2
Vietnamese Refugee Arrival by Year and State of Primary Migration, 1975–1978

State	1975	1976	1977	1978
Alabama	1,420	11	6	73
Alaska	74	0	7	14
Arizona	1,341	1	17	148
Arkansas	2,775	10	12	118
California	24,550	344	1,041	4,080
Colorado	1,988	15	58	241
Connecticut	1,129	5	37	145
Delaware	160	0	3	0
District of Columbia	839	3	28	212
Florida	5,629	12	106	401
Georgia	1,464	20	35	95
Guam	247	0	0	0
Hawaii	807	26	28	220
Idaho	306	0	7	9
Illinois	4,090	20	78	595
Indiana	1,924	42	45	122
Iowa	2,427	8	18	78
Kansas	1,902	0	30	176
Kentucky	985	11	11	98
Louisiana	4,268	8	271	496
Maine	388	2	5	23
Maryland	2,263	11	25	200
Massachusetts	1,195	2	0	147
Michigan	2,401	17	41	246
Minnesota	4,123	11	58	318
Mississippi	481	0	0	87
Missouri	3,180	3	40	208
Montana	214	1	5	26
Nebraska	1,311	3	26	96
Nevada	384	5	4	100
New Hampshire	166	0	3	0
New Jersey	1,709	0	10	86
New Mexico	1,124	9	60	147
New York	4,298	37	351	726
North Carolina	1,394	0	3	56
North Dakota	427	0	4	32
Ohio	3,117	4	16	131
Oklahoma	0	1	21	261

Table 2.2 (continued)

State	1975	1976	1977	1978
Oregon	1,322	1,902	1,250	821
Pennsylvania	2,469	3,223	2,259	1,243
Rhode Island	75	85	217	65
South Carolina	252	292	243	179
South Dakota	153	113	39	67
Tennessee	539	413	184	272
Texas	4,812	7,550	4,906	4,407
Utah	899	1,144	522	198
Vermont	12	61	22	10
Virginia	1,592	2,282	1,304	924
Washington	2,246	3,186	2,211	1,352
West Virginia	80	142	44	40
Wisconsin	492	499	331	248
Wyoming	59	39	12	13
Unknown	3	0	0	0
Total	63,020	83,654	57,673	37,085

Source: Appendix A from Strand and Jones, *Indochinese Refugees in America*, 1985.

up of extended families was that people were potentially sponsored to different parts of the country. Unless the sponsors were able and willing to sponsor an entire extended family, members of the same extended family were resettled according to the voluntary agencies' ability to match refugees with sponsors.

In addition, many of the social networks that formed while they were abandoning their homeland as well as in refugee camps were also temporarily disrupted. This forced the Vietnamese refugees to interact with, and depend on, the sponsors and the immediate environment for social and emotional support. In essence, the Vietnamese were deprived of the emotional, social, and psychological support generated from the extended family and also the support that was generated from shared culture, language, customs, and experience. They became isolated in their new "homes" and had to rely for support on sponsors who did not speak their language, understand their customs, or celebrate their culture.

Third, to minimize the strain put on local economies by the arrival of Vietnamese refugees, the federal government encouraged the U.S. sponsors to help the refugees to become financially independent as soon as possible by obtaining jobs. Therefore, in order to survive, many Vietnamese refugees had to accept jobs immediately. Consequently, the jobs they obtained were generally those of lower status than the ones they had in Vietnam or ones that required little or no skills. Most of these jobs were concentrated in the periphery economy or were service jobs that required no skills and little or no English proficiency. These were also low-paying jobs with little possibility for advancement and without medical benefits.

Accordingly, most Vietnamese refugees reported a decline in their families' socioeconomic status since their arrival in the United States. This decline is especially striking when they compare their current status to their socioeconomic standing in Vietnam before 1975 and the political changes. Parents of college students who came in the first period were reported to hold better jobs and occupations than those from the second period. For example, fathers who served as officers in the South Vietnamese Armed Forces now work as janitors at high schools; a former businessman is a dishwasher in an ethnic-owned restaurant; a former college professor drives a school bus; and a former high-ranking government official works as a low-level technician in a high-tech company. Similarly, many Vietnamese women were working for the first time outside the home as technicians or assemblers in high-technology industries, cooks, teachers' aids, cosmologists, office helpers, social workers, or maids.

After living for a period of time with their sponsors and adjusting to the new environment, many Vietnamese refugees began to relocate to different locations throughout the United States. They did not remain in the original place of their resettlement for a number of reasons. Weather played a significant role in the formation of a secondary migration (the voluntary migration of people after a few years of their initial resettlement by voluntary organizations) initiated by Vietnamese refugees. Weather conditions that exist in many parts of the United States were substantially different from those in Vietnam. In only a few states—California, Texas, and Florida—was the climate somewhat similar to that of Vietnam.

The 1980 United States Census Data on the Vietnamese Americans in the United States indicated that the most populated states were California with 34.78 percent, Texas with 11.34 percent, Louisiana with 4.43 percent, Virginia with 3.86 percent, Washington with 3.65 percent, Pennsylvania with 3.31 percent, and Florida with 2.89 percent (Table 2.3). Fifty percent of the entire Vietnamese refugee population lived in either California, Texas, or Louisiana. Almost two thirds (64.26 percent) lived in only seven states, including the aforementioned three states, plus Virginia (3.86 percent),

Table 2.3
Vietnamese Refugees' Arrival by Year and State of Primary Migration, 1979–1982

State	1979	1980	1981	1982
Alabama	409	324	280	194
Alaska	41	97	21	19
Arizona	574	681	300	191
Arkansas	437	577	329	196
California	21,067	29,630	21,111	11,313
Colorado	875	1,071	763	534
Connecticut	557	612	430	335
Delaware	35	44	23	10
District of Columbia	108	1,228	933	490
Florida	1,621	1,770	1,323	905
Georgia	698	1,079	1,358	870
Hawaii	1,428	1,113	577	407
Idaho	82	116	81	133
Illinois	2,191	2,600	1,531	1,102
Indiana	624	729	257	222
Iowa	695	726	495	281
Kansas	640	1,001	1,104	860
Kentucky	229	321	281	322
Louisiana	1,148	2,027	1,620	1,001
Maine	195	173	91	49
Maryland	683	944	452	296
Massachusetts	984	1,921	1,828	1,089
Michigan	1,163	1,525	754	462
Minnesota	1,724	2,107	1,132	807
Mississippi	284	330	205	201
Missouri	872	997	799	544
Montana	153	72	17	21
Nebraska	284	354	312	245
Nevada	372	410	157	86
New Hampshire	43	35	41	32
New Jersey	693	1,229	624	571
New Mexico	434	419	552	222
New York	2,835	3,328	2,439	856
North Carolina	792	922	399	345
North Dakota	117	48	99	36
Ohio	980	1,066	640	432
Oklahoma	978	1,097	768	567

Table 2.3 (continued)

State	1979	1980	1981	1982
Oregon	1,681	4	63	417
Pennsylvania	7,995	4	52	624
Puerto Rico	1	0	0	0
Rhode Island	0	0	0	26
South Carolina	221	5	27	9
South Dakota	842	0	18	29
Tennessee	579	1	18	182
Texas	1,148	65	388	1,491
Utah	9,789	1	0	142
Vermont	576	0	0	1
Virgin Islands	4,019	0	0	0
Virginia	4,157	0	33	355
Washington	4,116	1	132	431
West Virginia	214	0	0	5
Wisconsin	1,972	0	52	129
Wyoming	140	0	7	1
Unknown	158	0	0	0
Total	124,108	813	3,333	14,053

Source: Appendix A from Strand and Jones, *Indochinese Refugees in America*, 1985.

Author's note: The data reported in this appendix were obtained from the Center for Disease Control (CDC), as the Office of Refugee Resettlement (ORR) could not provide ethnic and state breakdowns. However, the CDC data were not complete for 1975. They contained only 109,000 records against an ORR figure of 129,792. To resolve this problem, the CDC figures for 1975 were adjusted upward in proportion to their original contribution to the CDC total so that a revised total of 129,792 could be shown. The assumption of this adjustment is that the missing records would be distributed in a manner identical to those that exist.

Washington (3.65 percent), Pennsylvania (3.31 percent), and Florida (2.89 percent).

As the harsh winter conditions hit large cities throughout the colder parts of the United States where Vietnamese refugees were initially resettled, the desire to find a location with a warmer climate and a Vietnamese community increased. Additionally, California's reputation for having a warm climate and an abundance of unskilled jobs, especially in San Jose's "Silicon Valley," Santa Ana, and San Diego, along with the existence of small Vietnamese communities in Los Angeles and San Jose, attracted people. A total of 43 percent of Vietnamese Americans who had migrated to Orange County, California, gave "climate" as their primary reason for migrating, whereas 22

Saigon Reform Church, Westminster, California, 1990. Courtesy of Hien Duc Do.

percent gave "job/finances/education" as their second reason, followed by "family nearby" with 13 percent (Baldwin, 1984). This secondary migration pattern is repeated often as many Vietnamese American communities have been established throughout the United States.

The latest census data (1990) on Vietnamese living in the United States indicate that those states in which the immigrants concentrated their secondary migration are still the most populated with Vietnamese Americans. Table 2.4 reveals that California, with 45.36 percent of the population, is still the state most preferred by the total number of Vietnamese immigrants living in the United States. Texas is still second at 11.27 percent. Washington, with 4.81 percent, and Virginia, with 3.30 percent, have moved ahead of Louisiana, with 2.85 percent. Florida, with 2.65 percent is still fifth whereas Pennsylvania is now sixth with 2.57 percent. These seven states together combine for almost 73 percent of the total number of Vietnamese immigrants living in the United States.

SUMMARY

The end of the Vietnam War compounded with the fear of the new Vietnamese communist government contributed to the large and sudden influx

Table 2.4
Vietnamese Population in the United States (1980) by State

State		%	State		%
Alabama	1,220	0.50	Montana	82	.03
Alaska	306	0.13	Nebraska	1,276	0.52
Arizona	1,756	0.72	Nevada	1,018	0.42
Arkansas	1,900	0.78	New Hampshire	136	0.06
California	85,238	34.78	New Jersey	2,846	1.16
Colorado	3,247	1.33	New Mexico	936	0.38
Connecticut	1,575	0.64	New York	5,849	2.39
Delaware	171	0.70	North Carolina	1,966	0.80
District of Columbia	435	0.18	North Dakota	288	0.12
Florida	7,077	2.89	Ohio	2,751	1.12
Georgia	2,339	0.96	Oklahoma	4,174	1.70
Hawaii	3,403	1.39	Oregon	5,743	2.35
Idaho	443	0.18	Pennsylvania	8,127	3.32
Illinois	6,287	2.57	Rhode Island	287	0.12
Indiana	2,137	0.87	South Carolina	1,113	0.45
Iowa	2,101	0.86	South Dakota	265	0.11
Kansas	3,331	1.32	Tennessee	1,158	0.47
Kentucky	1,461	0.60	Texas	27,791	11.34
Louisiana	10,853	4.43	Utah	1,991	0.81
Maine	260	0.11	Vermont	94	0.04
Maryland	4,162	1.70	Virginia	9,451	3.86
Massachusetts	2,847	1.16	Washington	8,933	3.66
Michigan	4,364	1.78	West Virginia	168	0.07
Minnesota	5,316	2.17	Wisconsin	1,699	0.69
Mississippi	1,477	0.60	Wyoming	43	0.02
Missouri	3,134	1.28	Total	245,025	100%

Source: 1980 U.S. Bureau of the Census, General Social and Economic Characteristics.

of Vietnamese refugees and immigrants to the United States since 1975. This chapter illustrated how the social, political, and economic conditions in the United States of America during the time of the Vietnamese refugees' arrival greatly affected the ways in which the U.S. federal government designed and implemented its refugee policies. That is, the Federal Government Dispersion Policy implemented under President Ford's administration was done with the intention of quickly assimilating Vietnamese refugees into the United States. However, despite the original intention of the federal government to disperse Vietnamese refugees throughout the United States, the

Vietnamese refugees initiated a secondary migration by themselves that resulted in their primary concentration in seven states.

As a result of the original pattern of resettlement, this secondary migration and the length of time since their first arrival in 1975, Vietnamese immigrants have been able to establish small communities throughout the United States, but concentrated in only a few states. Moreover, as a result of the Orderly Departure Program, the Humanitarian Operation Program, and the Homecoming Act of 1987, many former refugees are now able to sponsor immediate family members for immigration to the United States. This has contributed to the continuing influx of Vietnamese immigrants to the United States.

Most Vietnamese immigrants live in large metropolitan and urban areas. They tend to concentrate in the inner cities and ethnic enclaves. As mentioned earlier, California has the largest number of Vietnamese immigrants among the 50 states. Although data for the 1990 Standard Metropolitan Statistical Areas (SMSA) have not been released, the 1990 United States Census Data reveal that the cities in the state of California with the largest concentration of Vietnamese Americans are Westminster, Santa Ana, Long Beach, Los Angeles, San Jose, San Francisco, and San Diego. All recent research indicates that there do not seem to be any significant changes.

NOTE

1. Although relatively little money by today's standards, a Volkswagen Beetle sold for $1,899 in 1975. The average cost of a house was between $26,000 to $45,000.

3

Issues in the Vietnamese American Community

ISSUES IN THE EARLY RESETTLEMENT PERIOD

One of the characteristics of the history of the United States is that, with the exception of Native Americans, it is a history of immigrants. Although there have been numerous waves of immigration of people from all over the world, historians and sociologists have generally agreed on three distinct waves. The first wave of immigration to the United States took place early in the seventeenth century to 1860. Immigrants from this wave were primarily people from Northern and Western European countries. The second wave occurred between 1860 to 1920. Immigrants from this wave came to both the Atlantic and Pacific Coasts. Immigrants who arrived on Ellis Island, New York, were primarily from Southern and Eastern European countries. Immigrants who immigrated through Angel Island, California, arrived primarily from Asia. The third wave of immigration occurred as a result of the Immigration Act of 1965. Immigrants from this wave were admitted by two major criteria— occupational certification and family reunification. Members of this wave were given preference because they had specific skills needed in the economy. Others came to be reunited with their families. The majority of immigrants from this wave came from Latin America and Asia. The experiences of each immigrant group differed in the ways in which they were received and treated by those immigrants already established in the United States. As a result of this immigration history, one of the questions that social scientists have been, and continue to be, interested in is, "How is a new group of immigrants going to be incorporated into America?"

The transition from being a refugee group to being an immigrant group in the United States is the focus of this chapter. Of particular interest are the racial and ethnic conflicts that have occurred across the country when Vietnamese refugees first arrived and were resettled. In particular, our focus is on incidents that occurred in Seadrift, Texas, and along the Gulf Coast, in Denver, Colorado, and in Santa Ana, California. These incidents are among those that clearly indicate some prejudice and discrimination that have taken place against Vietnamese. These incidents will be examined in the context of trying to understand the dynamics of the Vietnamese refugees' relations with other racial and ethnic groups in America, why such incidents have occurred, what is similar or different about the Vietnamese American experience in relation to other racial minority groups in America, and U.S. reactions to Vietnamese as opposed to the feelings of the refugees themselves.

The analysis will use a theory of prejudice developed by historian Roger Daniels and sociologist Harry Kitano. Although they cannot explain the roots and causes of prejudice, they do explore the mechanics of prejudice. They view prejudice as "in-group" and "out-group" phenomena (Daniels and Kitano, 1970). In other words, for prejudice to take place there must be at least two groups ("two categories") with unequal power. In effect, the group with more power, that is, the superior group, designates the other group as the inferior group to be oppressed. According to this model, if there were more than two groups, other groups would be discriminated against, but not to the same extent.

Daniels and Kitano's theory focuses primarily on the ways in which the two-category system is maintained. They divide prejudice into four stages: informal stereotyping, discrimination, segregation, and the "extraordinary solution." The shift from one stage to the next represents an increase in the degree of seriousness in dealing with the inferior group by denying them access to resources or to formally sanction their activities. Daniels and Kitano suggest that in the discrimination stage, formal laws are proposed to deal with the inferior group, while the segregation stage involves threats to the physical safety of the group such as lynching and other warnings. In the final stage, the extraordinary solution, actions can take the form of apartheid, expulsion, or extermination.

In addition, Daniels and Kitano maintain that four major factors are influential in determining the level of threat that the majority group feels. These are color—the darker the skin color, the more prejudice; numbers—the larger the number, the more threatening the group; nationality—the associations of the country that one comes from; and culture—including all the cultural characteristics that threaten the majority group's sense of security.

The following section presents three different threats that the majority group in this country felt when Vietnamese refugees settled in their midst and the incidents that arose subsequently.

Economic Threat: Seadrift, Texas

In the highly publicized case of the white Texas fishermen versus the Vietnamese American fishermen, tensions between fishing rights erupted into physical confrontation in 1981. A white fisherman who had threatened some Vietnamese American fishermen was killed in self-defense on August 3, 1979. The townspeople were incensed by this incident. A long series of harassment took place in which Vietnamese boats and houses were firebombed.

A point of interest was that the Ku Klux Klan was found to be organizing against the Vietnamese immigrants and was actively training fifty-two white fishermen in survival training courses. They were using this racial incident as an organizing event to recruit and support people they thought might be sympathetic to their cause. The issue was then framed as one of racial differences between the parties involved and their physical and cultural dissimilarities.

There were many sources of conflict in this incident. There was the misunderstanding by the Texas fishermen of the money allocated to the sponsors to help resettle Vietnamese refugees. The sponsors thought the money was given to them to do with as they wished. Some Vietnamese thought the money should have gone directly to them and not to the U.S. sponsors. There was also misunderstanding in the fishing rights and fishing etiquette observed in the area. This was exacerbated by the rumors, true and otherwise, of exploitation, unfair treatment, and the thought of an emerging and developing large Vietnamese American fishing village in Louisiana. There was speculation that an entire Vietnamese fishing village was going to be transplanted there and that the Vietnamese fishermen were going to take over the entire fishing industry. The final straw that lead to the eruption of violence was the intense economic competition posed by the Vietnamese refugees. They were seen as being too successful at catching fish.

Two things stand out regarding this incident and others similar to it from around the country. First, there were basic differences in the cultural and fishing practices of the two parties involved. As recent newcomers to the United States, the Vietnamese fishermen may not have been aware of the need for licenses, the legal and illegal use of certain equipment, and the etiquette involved in fishing. Second, the strongest resentment resulted from the fact that Vietnamese fishermen were thought to work too hard. Since they wanted to establish themselves economically and to provide for their families, Vietnamese fishermen worked long hours and used family labor to help them in this process. As a common cultural practice, each member of the family contributed to the demanding work. In chasing the American dream of becoming economically independent and self-sufficient, Vietnamese fishermen found themselves at odds with the local residents. For example, since they did not have the money to buy new boats, they purchased old vessels and refurbished them to keep the cost to a minimum. Also, because they were not yet citizens of the United States, they could not buy the larger and more technologically advanced boats that can go further out to catch the more desirable types of fish that would have made fishing more lucrative. Consequently, they concentrated in areas where they were least likely to face competition from local fishermen. Nevertheless, they were blamed for some of the difficulties faced by the fishing industry. In essence, the Vietnamese fishermen were using the same principles of hard work in all types of difficult and dangerous weather conditions in order to catch fish and keeping long hours that the American fishermen respected, but they were resented for doing it to an extreme. In sum, the basis of the racial tension was the economic threat the townspeople felt toward their livelihood.

The form in which these instances of prejudice took place is interesting. There were rumors that not only were there more Vietnamese refugees in the town than there really were, but that many more were coming. E. J. Cunningham, a city council member, was able to mobilize feelings against the refugees by speculating that an additional one million Vietnamese refugees were due to arrive by the end of 1979 and that most were going to be resettled along the gulf coast (Oster, "Texas Town Turns against Refugees" 1979). The reality was that there was already a quota set by the federal government, and that according to the Dispersion policy, most people were going to be relocated in other states throughout the country. There were also rumors that Vietnamese refugees were given more than their share of social services by the government. For example, the Small Business Administration was supposedly providing interest-free or low-interest loans to Vietnamese refugees so that they could buy boats, and the refugees purportedly did not have to pay taxes on their wages. Although these rumors were never substantiated, they nevertheless succeeded in creating an atmosphere of fear and resentment in the local white residents.

In addition, attributes were given to the refugees that portrayed them as evil. Vietnamese refugees were viewed and described in the local newspapers as being "sneaky, bellicose, unsanitary people who lived through 100 years of warfare to emerge with little respect for human life" (Gillan, 1979). Again, these were some of the same characteristics that have been attributed to other Asian Americans since their first arrivals to the United States in the 1800s.

Ultimately, the incidents were not limited to physical confrontations but also included legal actions. Local fishermen successfully lobbied and petitioned the Texas legislature to ban Vietnamese refugees from holding commercial fishing licenses. In the end, the events that took place between Vietnamese refugees and the townspeople in Seadrift, Texas, followed the three stages of prejudice as theorized by Daniels and Kitano.

Sexual Threats: Santa Ana, California

The case of three Vietnamese men convicted of rape in Santa Ana, California, on April 1981 stands out as another fascinating model to study race and interethnic relations. Two women walking alone at night were approached by a carload of four young men asking for directions. One or more of the men left the car, grabbed the women, pushed them into the waiting car, and sped away. A gun or knife was used to threaten the women and, later, the women were raped in an orange grove.

Of course, the seriousness of their actions cannot be accepted or condoned in any society. However, the most controversial aspect of this case is the sentences given to the defendants. On charges of gang-raping these women, the rapists were given sentences of unprecedented length. Two of the defendants were given a sentence of 118 ½ years each, while the third man was sentenced to 100 ½ years. Since they were not given the possibility of early parole, they will spend between sixty to eighty years in prison. Thus, the three men will not be eligible for parole until well into their eighties.

The severity of the sentences touched off controversy in California. The perpetrators received sentences more severe than individuals convicted of manslaughter and murder. The *Santa Ana Register*, the local newspaper, thought the sentence to be too severe and proclaimed it "cruel and unusual punishment" and proffered that "the question must be asked if the penalty in any way matches the crime" (*Santa Ana Register*, 1981). If this case is viewed in the context of history, race, and ethnic relations, the question as to why these men received such a severe sentence might be better understood.

Although presiding Judge Briseno did not respond, the presiding judge of Orange County's Superior Court, Judge Rickles, did. He said that "in VIETNAM [original emphasis], they [the defendants] would have gotten the death sentence" (KFWB, 1981). What is interesting about Judge Rickles' response is that it seems to indicate that, at least in his mind, the sentences were clearly justified because of the nature of the defendants' background, not the crimes committed. In other words, they were convicted of the crime because they were guilty, but the sentence given was because they were Vietnamese, and not because of the crimes they committed. In short, the criteria for passing judgment on these Vietnamese men and the crimes they committed were not the same criteria that would have been used if they were "Americans."

The issue of interracial sexual relations has always been at the center of controversy in the history of the United States. Historically, numerous antimiscegenation laws throughout the United States, including the state of California, have been passed. In California these laws prohibited the "intermarriage of white persons with Chinese, Negroes, mulattos, or persons of mixed blood, descended from a Chinaman or negro from the third generation, inclusive" (Chan, 1991, p. 60). The laws were not declared unconstitutional by the Supreme Court of the United States until as recently as 1948. A study done by Susan Brownmiller on conviction rates for interracial rape found that African Americans received the stiffest sentences for raping white women (Brownmiller, 1975).

This case is important in understanding race and ethnic relations in the United States for the following reasons: First, the Vietnamese broke an American taboo, which resulted in swift, decisive, and severe retribution. Second, the incident contradicted the image of the Asian American male stereotype as being passive and emasculated. Third, the case resulted in blatant discriminatory actions through a legitimate U.S. institution, the legal system.

Threats to Other Minority Groups: Charlotte, North Carolina, and Denver, Colorado

Daniels and Kitano argue that those in the superior position of the "two-category" system need to feel superior to other identifiable groups. This identification serves the purpose of keeping the other groups that are subject to discrimination "working harder" because they might feel as if they are much closer to succeeding within the existing social system. In effect, there is an established racial hierarchy that each group will strive to rise to the top. This tactic is also known as "divide and conquer" or "preferential treatment." By shifting the focus to other groups, the superior group is able to deflect criticisms against itself while simultaneously succeeding at maintaining the perception of an open system.

The following discussion examines how this identification manifested itself through incidents in two states. The first incident, in Charlotte, North Carolina, occurred when African Americans felt the Vietnamese refugees received preferential treatment in a lower-income housing track called Grier Heights. Vietnamese were seen as allowed to move into the housing project at the expense of many other African Americans who had been presumably on a waiting list for a long time. African Americans resented the fact that "the Vietnamese did not die in World War I and World War II as our fathers and grandfathers died for this country. We had to work hard for what we have. Now you want to give the Vietnamese all the things we have worked for" (Oster, 1979). Fortunately, that incident was limited only to harsh words. African Americans were expressing the underlying understanding that a new group has to pay its dues like all the other groups before it can harvest and enjoy the benefits from this country. As Americans who have served in both World Wars, helped build the country with their labor, and suffered continual discrimination, African Americans begrudged Vietnamese immigrants for receiving preferential treatment, especially since Vietnamese have not contributed to the overall development of the United States of America. They felt that the federal government was willing to provide for Vietnamese who were strangers to this country, while African Americans who are longstanding citizens have not received the same support. The actions by the federal government violated the sense of fairness and highlighted the continued mistreatment of the African American community.

In Denver, Colorado, ethnic and racial antagonisms went beyond harsh words. On August 20, 1979, two Chicano youths robbed a Vietnamese family in their own home. A Vietnamese boy in the same housing project apprehended the robbers. Community residents who witnessed the incident reported that the Vietnamese boy beat the robbers. The next morning, in retaliation for the beating, non-Vietnamese residents threw rocks at the Vietnamese households. Shortly thereafter, out of fear of further physical violence and for the safety of their families, fourteen Vietnamese families left the South Lincoln Park housing project. This incident aroused national attention and publicity.

A study conducted soon after the incident in that neighborhood found that the overriding sentiment on the part of the Chicanos was that Vietnamese refugees were receiving preferential treatment in the areas of housing, health care, education, and jobs. For example, in the area of housing, Chicano residents observed that the South Lincoln Project took Vietnamese refugees despite a long waiting list comprised mostly of Chicanos. With respect to health care, Chicano residents noticed that bilingual speakers and people who understood the special problems of Vietnamese refugees were hired to provide direct services to them. This caused resentment on the part of Chicano residents who felt that there were not enough bilingual Spanish speakers to address their children's needs. They resented the fact that Vietnamese refugees were receiving social services that their own children were not receiving. In education, before the arrival of Vietnamese refugees, there were general cutbacks of all services in areas like Headstart and adult education that were affecting the larger community. However, when Vietnamese refugees arrived, bilingual immigrants were hired to provide services for them. The resentment arose from residents' questioning where the additional funds had came from, and the feeling that if services were provided to the Vietnamese community it would be at the expense of the already scarce bilingual resources available to Chicano children.

Additional resentment from the Chicano community was caused by the mass media's stereotypes of Vietnamese immigrant children as being high achievers eager to learn. In effect, the stereotypes implied that their children were not as eager to learn or high achievers. In the area of economic competition, Vietnamese refugees were seen as receiving help that enabled them to find higher-paying jobs than Chicanos even though they did not necessarily come with higher levels of skills from Vietnam. Finally, resentment leftover from the Vietnam War affected Chicano attitudes adversely, especially for those who had lost relatives in the war. It was not uncommon for people to resent Vietnamese refugees personally for many of their own social and personal problems, including the loss of loved ones during the long Vietnam War. This sentiment is understandable since there was a disproportionate number of African American and Chicano soldiers killed during the war.

This case is similar to the incident in Charlotte, North Carolina. As a result of the influx of refugees, local residents felt deprived of their rights to receive services and benefits that rightfully belonged to them as long-standing citizens. They also perceived themselves as victims of the continued uneven distribution of scarce resources. They could not comprehend how it was possible for the federal government to provide services for the refugees when it had argued that there were not enough funds to meet the requests of the local residents. Finally, local residents did not think that the Vietnamese refugees should receive special privileges, when they were the ones who had been in the United States for many generations and their communities had contributed to the overall development of the country.

The greatest amount of antagonism between Vietnamese refugees and other racial minority groups seemed to occur for three reasons. First, Vietnamese refugees appear to have received preferential treatment from the federal government. Second, since there were limited resources, there was a perceived competition for these resources. It was seen as a matter of survival;

that is, if one group received the scarce resources, then the other group would not receive them. Third, the cultural differences between these groups were so distinct that communication rarely took place and stereotypes easily developed. Interestingly, these sentiments were also true among other Asian American groups when the Vietnamese refugees first arrived. They too were afraid that some of the gains made in the past through difficult struggles, as well as the social services they were receiving, would be cut back.

What can be discerned from these three case studies? An interesting facet in the case of Vietnamese immigrants is that there are compelling reasons to place them in the category of "model minority." Although in terms of skin pigmentation Vietnamese immigrants are similar to white Americans, they have features distinct enough to make them easily identifiable. In addition, the cultural values that they possess are similar to the dominant American culture—that is, working hard and obeying authority. In short, they possess some of the characteristics valued in America.

It is, however, the other two variables in Daniels and Kitano's theory—number and nationality—that perhaps render the potentially positive factors ineffectual and, in fact, transform the positive into the negative. The large number of Vietnamese refugees and Southeast Asian refugees that has come within a very short period of time has been dramatic and noticeable. For example, between 1975 and 1981, the number increased dramatically from 4,000 to 465,000. Additionally, the extensive amount of media coverage had a dual effect. On one hand, it served to mobilize the humanitarian support of the American public to reach out and help Vietnamese refugees, while on the other hand, the media also lead the American public to believe that there were many more refugees than there really were. Again, the larger the number is perceived to be, the more the new group is seen as a threat.

The other variable, that of nationality, was also influenced by the mass media. In essence, the media highlighted and reinforced some of the attitudes Americans had toward the Vietnam War. The media also pointed to the many divisions created within society because of the war and other social and political issues. Again, there is the tendency to equate Vietnamese with the only war the United States has ever lost.

The three incidents reported above that took place in Texas, Colorado, and California bring to the forefront the dynamics of race relations and the incorporation of a new group in America. Vietnamese refugees, despite not seeing themselves as a minority group shortly after their arrival, were soon treated as one. According to Daniels and Kitano's four levels of racial prejudice, the Vietnamese are well past stage one, that of simple informal stereotyping. The second level, discrimination in the legal arena, has been seen in attempts to get city councils to stop issuing business licenses to Vietnamese immigrants and in differential treatment in sentencing of Vietnamese Americans as seen in the Santa Ana case. As for the third level, threats to physical safety, there have been incidents of firebombing, physical assaults, and Ku Klux Klan organizing. The final stage, that of "extraordinary solutions," would have to have be triggered by some major event such as war or riots. This stage is unlikely to occur under present circumstances in American society because of all the gains made by the struggles of the Civil Rights Movement and other social movements in recent years.

However, unlike the entrance of other immigrant groups to the United States the entrance of the Vietnamese immigrants into minority group status in the United States is marked with controversy in part because of the manner in which resettlement policy was carried out. Even though money was given to volunteer agencies, it was not given to those institutions that the refugees would eventually make use of, including housing and schools. Thus, Vietnamese were seen as providing a vast amount of economic competition while at the same time receiving preferential treatment.

The future interaction between Vietnamese and other racial and ethnic groups will be interesting to observe and will depend on two important variables. With a growing public perception that Vietnamese immigrants are entering the status of a minority group it is more likely that other groups, including those who were formerly antagonistic, will become more supportive. In addition, language acquisition, methods of interaction, and means of survival will inevitably be learned by the immigrants and it will help form support networks. As a result, they will be better able to organize and address some of the concerns and issues of their community.

RECENT ISSUES

Housing

One of the social characteristics of Vietnamese immigrants is that of the extended family. Unlike American families, traditional Vietnamese families tend not only to be larger but also to include extended family members. It is common to find parents, children, grandparents, and unmarried aunts and uncles living in the same house. Consequently, one area where there is a mismatch between Vietnamese customs and American customs is in housing. In a study of Vietnamese households in San Diego, California, it was reported that Vietnamese American households average 5.5 individuals as compared to 2.7 in the average U.S. household (Rumbaut, 1988).

Despite the Federal Government Dispersion policy, which broke up extended families to make the sponsorship process more manageable, the fact remained that the average Vietnamese family was larger than the average American family. This became even more evident as refugees left their original settlement and migrated to areas with a larger Vietnamese population. As a result of this process, many extended families were reunited, and the personal, social, and emotional support network was reestablished and the family size became larger once again.

This family reunification led to some problems with respect to finding affordable housing in the American housing market. In the 1980s, throughout the United States, low-cost housing had for many years been less profitable to build and operate than luxury housing or commercial construction. The housing construction industry has been responding to general U.S. trends leading to a de-emphasis on the construction of rental properties designed for large households. In addition, many rental units had been converted into condominiums, and most apartment and housing units do not have more than three bedrooms. If strict housing regulations were applied, it was difficult for Vietnamese immigrants to find affordable apartments large enough to accommodate the family.

David Haines, an anthropologist who studied the question of the Vietnamese family as faced with the American housing market, suggested possible solutions. One solution was to ease the restriction on "one person, one room" that seemed to dominate housing management policies—a policy designed to prevent overcrowding. The other solution was private ownership of homes, which would then allow owners to determine their own arrangements (Haines, 1980). Since it is unlikely that the principle of "one person, one room" will change, the consequence will be that many Vietnamese will be forced to live illegally in these housing complexes. The second solution of private ownership is more likely to become possible as Vietnamese immigrants reside longer in the United States.

Since 1975 when Vietnamese arrived in the refugee camps in the United States, the housing situation has steadily improved. In California in 1995, the number of houses sold to Vietnamese with the last name Nguyen, the most common Vietnamese last name, ranked nineteenth on a list of home sales by last name (Perkins, 1995). This number seems to suggest that, similar to other Americans, Vietnamese Americans consider homeownership an important goal to achieve. However, given the previous discussion on housing, the more intriguing issues are how many people were required to pool resources for a down payment and the number of people that live in a given house. In Santa Clara County, California, for example, more than two families commonly share a house, with other rooms rented out for additional income. Finally, though home ownership is important, it is only secondary to education with respect to influence in determining the level of success of an immigrant group.

Youth and Gang Activities and Education

In a *Los Angeles Times* survey conducted in 1994 (June 13), 41 percent of Vietnamese Americans living in six counties in California, including Los Angeles County, Orange County, Riverside County, San Bernardino County, San Diego County, and Ventura County, considered gangs and crimes as the most serious problems facing their community. Although Vietnamese American communities throughout the United States have different characteristics, in general, this sentiment is an accurate reflection of their collective viewpoint. Some of the better-known Vietnamese gangs in the United States are Asian Boys, U-Boys, Young Asian, Nips, A.W.A. (Asian with attitudes), the Panthers, A.K.A. (Asian kick ass), Oriental Boys, the Dragon, and B.T.K. (Born to Kill—taken from a logo used by American GIs during the Vietnam War). Although there are few statistics indicating the degree of gang activities, researchers have been able to identify some of the main characteristics of gang life.

In general, most gang members tend to be young males between fifteen and twenty-four years old. Gang members are usually mobile and travel in groups of six or more, moving from state to state. They comprise those individuals who have generally not been academically successful in school and feel alienated from the larger society. These individuals see little point to achieving success in the conventional way. That is, because of their inability to stay in school and their lack of vocational skills, they do not see the necessity for working hard to earn a living. They do not necessarily think of future plans and goals. Primarily, they live for the moment. Until recently, most of their crimes targeted Vietnamese American communities, and thus their victims had been other Vietnamese Americans.

Although Vigil and Yun (1990) have suggested that unlike African American or Latino gangs, Vietnamese gangs do not have any colors, carry any names, or guard any turf, they have developed different mechanisms by which to identify themselves. They identify themselves through specific tattoos or cigarette burns. The tattoos generally have Asian motifs in the form of tigers, dragons, snakes, or simply five dots inconspicuously placed on their body. The five dots represent *tinh, tien, tu, toi,* and *thu* (love, money, prison, sin, and revenge). One of the most common ways in which they operate their day-to-day activities is to burglarize commercial establishments and residential homes and quickly escape law enforcement authorities by fleeing to different Vietnamese American communities throughout the United States. As a result of this pattern, Vietnamese gangs tend to live either in motels ("mo's") or rented rooms. This has made it difficult for authorities to accurately determine their population.

Even though there are numerous paths to delinquency, one of the reasons young Vietnamese Americans began to participate in gang activities was as a result of their inability to adjust to life in the United States. For some recent arrivals or students from the second immigration period, the formal education they received in Vietnam was very limited and inadequate. After the war, the Vietnamese communist government restricted access to education and many young people were unable to continue their education. Most former military officers and people associated with the old Vietnamese government were sent to re-education camps, a euphemism for political prisons or labor camps, for many years after 1975. These policies negatively impacted the lives of many families, especially the younger people.

Mr. Ngo,[1] a former colonel in the South Vietnamese army, who received a college education and professional degrees before the end of the war, spent thirteen years in a prison labor camp in the deep jungle of North Vietnam before he was finally released in 1988. While in prison, all seven of his children were denied access to higher education and to many occupations for which they were trained or had the skills and qualifications in Vietnam. For example, one of his sons, Binh, attended the University of Saigon and had graduated as an engineer prior to the end of the war in 1975. However, as a result of his father's role as a military officer during the war, Binh was not allowed to work as an engineer. His sister experienced the same fate. Mai Huong received her degree as an elementary school teacher but was not allowed to teach. She was forced to find a new occupation as a vendor in the local market. Two of Ngo's other children are working as cyclo drivers in Ho Chi Minh City. However, Ngo's two oldest sons, both of whom were in the military during the war, fared better. They escaped Vietnam in 1980 and managed to immigrate to the United States as political refugees. After their initial resettlement in a city on the East Coast, both brothers managed to find jobs as machinists in an industrial company. After living in the United States for more than five years, they passed the citizenship examination and became U.S. citizens. The two brothers were then eligible to apply and to sponsor their parents to immigrate to the United States under the Orderly Departure Program in 1991. Unfortunately, the two brothers were unable to sponsor some of the other younger siblings because these siblings were married with families of their own. Immigration laws prohibit the sponsorship of married siblings for immigration to the United States.

Additionally, if the recent arrivals were refugees and spent a few years in one of the refugee camps throughout Southeast Asia (such as Hong Kong, Thailand, Malaysia, and the Philippines) prior to their resettlement in the United States, the education they received in the camps was primarily survival or conversational English, not formal education. Consequently, it would be natural for them to fall farther and farther behind in their formal education. Once in the United States, they are confronted with an educational system that places students in grade levels according to their age, regardless of their educational background. The result is that a fourteen-year-old girl is placed in ninth grade without much thought to her language proficiency or educational background. It is hardly surprising that many students find themselves lost in school, not just because of the lack of English proficiency but because they do not have the necessary skills to compete on the same grade level as someone else their age.

Hoai Nguyen, an Amerasian woman, the product of a U.S. serviceman and a Vietnamese woman, is an example of an individual who traveled this route through the American educational system. She has never met her biological father and was adopted by Mrs. Nga, a Vietnamese woman who did not have any children. Since Hoai was Amerasian and thus a reminder of the enemy of the Vietnam War, the Vietnamese communist government did not allow her to continue with her education after 1975. Her formal education stopped at the third-grade level. Similar to most other Amerasians, she felt unwanted by that society and was ostracized by other Vietnamese because of her mixed heritage. Hoai was forced to abandon her education and began peddling in the street markets with her mother in Ho Chi Minh City.

Hoai's life changed drastically due to passage of the Amerasian Immigration Act of 1982. As a result of her biracial heritage and her physical characteristics, it was obvious she was Amerasian. After spending months filling out the necessary paperwork and a series of interviews, Hoai was finally able to leave Vietnam in 1984 at the age of sixteen. Her family, which included her mother and her older brother, spent seven months in a refugee camp in the Philippines before finally immigrating to the United States. She was sponsored by an older uncle and resettled in Seattle, Washington. Hoai finally arrived in the United States as a seventeen-year-old teenager in May of 1985. Immediately upon arrival, she was put into the eleventh grade in the local high school. Because of her lack of formal education in Vietnam, she asked her counselor to transfer her and allow her to take English as a Second Language class. Despite all these efforts, she was unable to keep up with the demanding homework and flunked out of school. Shortly thereafter Hoai went to work as an assembler in a high tech company in Seattle. She later became involved with a man who participated in some illegal activities and found herself in trouble with the law. Although she was found innocent of the same crimes committed by her partner, Hoai was nevertheless sentenced to three years probation. While serving this sentence, she is enrolled at a community college and is trying to rebuild her life in order to provide for her two children. Hoai is an example of a student who had difficulty because she did not have the skills and education necessary to be put immediately into the educational system.

In addition to problems resulting from the educational system, Vietnamese students also face other challenges while attending schools. Besides the feeling of not belonging to the schools, some Vietnamese American students report being verbally harassed or physically threatened by other students in schools. Since Vietnamese Americans have generally resettled in large urban areas and tend to live in poor neighborhoods, young Vietnamese students face verbal and/or physical harassment from teenagers of other racial or ethnic groups. In large metropolitan cities such as San Jose, California; Boston; Westminster, California; and New York City, it is common to read newspaper reports and see television accounts of racial conflicts between Vietnamese youth and Latino youth, African American youth, Filipino youth, and Cambodian youth. Although the report from the U.S. Commission on Civil Rights in 1986 already drew attention to the problem of bigotry and violence against Asian Americans, this problem continued to plague Asian American students. In the 1992 report, the Commission on Civil Rights again emphasized the degree of racial tensions in public schools for Asian immigrants and how detrimental it is to their well-being.

In general, since recently arrived Vietnamese American youths do not have a strong command of the English language at school, they would usually spend time with others in the same situation, primarily other Vietnamese students. Understandably, since they are most comfortable speaking in their own language, they would speak to each other and interact with one another in their native language. This oftentimes lead to tensions with non-Vietnamese youths. Since Vietnamese American youths are generally not understood and are perceived to be making fun of or disrespecting other students, racial and ethnic conflicts sometimes occur. The result is that Vietnamese American youths oftentime find themselves made fun of, verbally harassed, called FOB ("fresh off the boat"), and beaten by other youths. Although Vietnamese youths can walk away from these situations and sometimes do, this action is usually seen as a sign of weakness and frequently only invites more abuse. Therefore, in order to protect themselves, many Vietnamese youths have resorted to forming small groups that often rely on physical fights as a means of protecting themselves and to minimize possible future confrontations. However, when these Vietnamese youths fight back, they tend to be merciless, because for them fighting is a survival skill that they had learned during the demanding and treacherous journey to America. This would be true even for those youths who did not experience the long and difficult journey to America, because they have been exposed to, and are familiar with, the "community collective memory." This collective memory is a set of stories testifying to the horrible and violent living conditions in Vietnam after the war horror, and the dangerous, frightful, and harrowing journeys that many people have had to endure to come to the United States in search of freedom. The stories are passed on from person to person within the Vietnamese American community through the telling and re-telling of personal incidents, newspaper articles, plays, short stories, books, and cultural legends. These stories are deeply embedded in the collective memory of the Vietnamese American community because everyone has gone through a similar ordeal or knows someone who went through the ordeal.

In 1995 a member of the Asian Brother gang recalled many fights where a member of his gang was fighting because he was provoked and, though much smaller than his counterpart, physically beat up the other student. For some Vietnamese youths who are not gang members but are caught fighting, this could lead them to the wrong path—that of juvenile delinquency. Due to the fact that these youths are not able to clearly explain to school officials the reasons that led to the fight, they are wrongly labeled as troublemakers and given the maximum penalty. The punishment they receive is seemingly unfair to them because the other students receive a less severe penalty simply because they are better able to express and explain themselves. In most areas where there is a large concentration of Vietnamese Americans, there are not enough Vietnamese school counselors or teachers who are able to speak to and for the immigrant youths. This situation could lead to a vicious cycle that begins at school, shifts to parental criticisms in the home, and might end with the student dropping out of school and joining a gang for protection and revenge.

As for the Vietnamese parents, in order to survive economically, many have to work two or sometimes three jobs. Since they do not have the necessary skills or the English proficiency to obtain high-paying jobs, their jobs are often low paying with few benefits and little opportunity for career advancement. Working long hours to provide for their families, these parents often do not have the time to understand their children's concerns and difficulties. Children are left home by themselves while the parents are busy working. Many times parents rely on the older children to take care of and provide guidance for the younger children. Moreover, without adequate knowledge of the educational system in the United States and the roles that parents may play, many parents generally assume that the schools are taking care of their children. As a result of the language barrier or lack of time, many do not participate in parent-teacher associations or attend conferences with the teachers. Additionally, some parents tend to believe the model minority myth perpetuated in the mass media, that Asian Pacific American students are extremely good students who excel academically and do not face the same problems as other teenagers. As such, parents sometimes have unrealistic expectations that their children should be doing well in school, especially given the tremendous sacrifices that they have made to bring them to the United States and given the long hours they have to work in order to provide a home for the children.

A manifestation of these social and cultural events is the increasing generation gap that developed as a result of the newcomers' struggle to survive in the United States. Children have become increasingly undisciplined and disrespectful toward their parents. Parents find themselves unable to relate to or even to speak with their children. Ms. Nguyen, a social worker and counselor working with Vietnamese American youths in San Jose, California, observes these problems in her counseling sessions with Vietnamese teenagers and their parents. In 1996, she reported many cases, including that of Maria, a thirteen-year-old girl who was referred to her for counseling after numerous incidents of running away from home and being apprehended by the police. The court required the mother, Mrs. Tran, to attend family counseling sessions with her in order to help resolve some of the conflicts. The primary conflicts revolved around the lack of communication between mother and child, the generation differences, conflicts over cultural and gender roles, and conflicts over school expectations. Both mother and daughter found themselves caught in a difficult situation. Mrs. Tran married a traditional Vietnamese husband who did not take part in helping raise the family and was primarily interested in his work and his friends. He also expected his wife to be a traditional Vietnamese woman, one who was responsible for taking care of the children and for maintaining the home. Maria felt that her parents were too strict and too traditional in wanting her to be a certain type of daughter: a daughter who does not question her parents, one who excels academically, and one who helps around the beauty shop and at home. She wanted more freedom. Although sympathetic to her daughter and the different pressures she felt, Mrs. Tran had a difficult time negotiating her new role in this society. On one hand, she was responsible for the upbringing of her daughter without the help and support of her husband, and, on the other hand, she was trying to accommodate the needs of her daughter who was also caught between two different cultures.

Ms. Nguyen also shared other incidents where dozens of Vietnamese youths, ranging from fourteen to seventeen in age, have run away from home and are currently living in a freeway overpass. Most of these youths have dropped out of school without their parents' knowledge and are spending time in public parks during the day smoking, sleeping, talking, or playing games while their parents are at work. They have developed an intricate system of support among themselves where one or two of the group members who are still on good terms with their parents are able to provide food, access to bathrooms for showers, and sometimes a place to sleep. Mr. Pham, a counselor who reaches out to these troubled youths, was amazed at their ability to hide their friends and their activities from their parents. As an example, Mr. Pham cites how they are able to have seven to ten youths sleeping in a person's room during the night, all take showers in the morning and then leave, seemingly without the parents' knowledge that there were that many people in their own house. Although not dangerous at the moment, these youths are in a precarious position because they are not receiving a high school education and have no discernible skills with which to provide for themselves in the future.

Joining a gang, or at least living the life of a gangster, can be very appealing and attractive for young people. Movies from Asia, especially those imported from Hong Kong, have generally depicted the life of a gangster as a very attractive and seductive underworld where money, women, and drugs are abundant. The Hong Kong video gangsters mythos are evident in words that many Vietnamese gang members have tattooed on their bodies: Love, Money, Prison, Sin, Revenge. Likewise, the success of these gangs is easily observable in a small community where gangsters can be seen dressing well, driving nice cars, eating at nice restaurants, and surrounded by beautiful young people.

Since the gangs know the fear and apprehension that exists in these communities, they can take advantage of the situation by asserting their power through intimidation and the use of physical force or violence. In general, there are several reasons for Vietnamese gangs' "success" in carrying out criminal activities within their own community. First and foremost, their ability to get information regarding a household, i.e., where cash, jewelry, gold, and other valuables are hidden and who will be home at what time of day. Because of the unpredictibility and instability of financial institutions in Vietnam throughout Vietnam's history, but especially during the war, and the tendency for people to conduct business transactions with cash or gold, Vietnamese Americans generally keep their savings, jewelry, gold, and other valuables at home. This is a well-known practice and custom used throughout the community but especially with the older generation (increasingly, younger Vietnamese Americans who have lived in the United States for a while are more likely to use banks). Unfortunately, this Vietnamese cultural practice of keeping large sums of money and jewelry at home is also well known by gang members. Gang members will seek out and befriend a younger member of the family that they are planning to rob and stake out the residence before actually committing the robbery. They are skillful at identifying youths that are alienated from school, unhappy with their family situation, and are easily seduced with friendships and material rewards. The gangs will provide the troubled youth with a sense of belonging to a "family" that is absent because the parents are working long hours. They will invest their time and money by taking the youth out to play in billiard halls, to hang out and dine in coffee shops, and to provide nice clothes in order to gain the confidence of this individual. They might also use psychological tactics by pointing out how alienated, unhappy, and unimportant he is and how little respect he receives from his parents. As a result of this interaction, trust and confidence will develop over a short period of time and important information regarding the family routines, the secret hiding places, and other crucial and relevant information will be extracted from these "informers." This will then lead to a swift and successful home invasion.

The second reason for the success of these gangs is that they rely on the general distrust Vietnamese Americans have for police and other law enforcement authorities. This attitude toward the police and authorities is deeply rooted and can be traced back to past experiences in Vietnam when police and the law enforcement authority were not seen as trustworthy institutions or capable of enforcing law and order. These institutions were generally seen as corrupt and not serving the needs of the common person. This apprehension is sometimes further exacerbated by some Vietnamese Americans' need to conceal some of the savings they have accumulated by working in the underground economy. They are afraid of jeopardizing some social service benefits (for example, social security income, welfare, Medicare, Aid to Families with Dependent Children) they might be receiving. This fear is so rampant that law enforcement officials estimate that as many as 50 percent of residential robberies are not reported by the victims (Barber, 1987). There is also a well-founded fear of reprisal by the gang members since many people believe that the police cannot protect them all the time. Living in a small community, there are many rumors and evidence of the retaliations inflicted by gang members in the forms of physical assaults and destruction of personal property.

In the case of the more recent arrivals, there is also the question of the language barrier and their understanding of the judicial system and law enforcement agencies. Since they are unfamiliar with the judicial system as well as law enforcement agencies, the more recent immigrants are less likely to report to these agencies and thereby expose their vulnerability to these types of crimes.

More recently, Vietnamese gangs have expanded the scope of their criminal activities. Instead of primarily targeting other Vietnamese Americans, they have begun to participate in more organized, increasingly violent crimes involving larger sums of money. Throughout the country, but primarily concentrated in California, Massachusetts, and New York, the Federal Bureau of Investigation has partnered with the local police and other federal agencies, including the Internal Revenue Service and the Federal Bureau of Alcohol, Tobacco and Firearms to expose and break the so-called high-tech crime rings. These crimes involve stealing computer chips in the United States and selling them on the black market in Asia. In the last few years, numerous undercover operations have been carried out jointly by the FBI and local law enforcement agencies to try to curb the increase in the number of violent crimes, including computer heists, gun sales, and drug trafficking. Oftentimes, the amount of money involved in these types of crimes ranges in the millions of dollars and involves hundreds of people throughout the country.

Religious Rights

One of the fascinating events that took place from 1986 until 1997 in San Jose, California, was that of the fight of a group of Vietnamese American Catholics to have their own "personal parish." The controversial event began when the so-called dissidents wanted to have a parish based on a common national identity instead of the traditional geographical boundaries. Since Vietnamese Americans lived throughout the city of San Jose, the dissidents argued that it was logical for them to have their own parish because of the number of people attending church services every Sunday. They also opposed the appointment of Father Paul Luu Dinh Duong as their local pastor because Father Duong supported the bishop's decision not to establish a Vietnamese parish at that time. The dissidents' argument was that a mission is only a temporary institution that the Catholic Church, if it so chooses, can eliminate at any time. A personal parish is a more permanent institution.

Duc Vien Temple, San Jose, California, 1998. Photo courtesy of Hien Duc Do.

Bishop DuMaine was against the establishment of a personal parish on the grounds that Vietnamese Americans have not demonstrated their economic self-sufficiency. The Bishop also argued that there were sufficient Masses in Vietnamese provided by Vietnamese priests in many Catholic churches throughout the city. This debate continued for the dissidents because they argued that other parishes have been established without these economic conditions, most notably in Texas and Louisiana. As a result of this disagreement between Bishop DuMaine, who represents the Catholic Diocese of San Jose, and the dissenters, after much legal litigation, the dissenters bought and operated their tiny chapel from the diocese in 1986. Although not officially recognized by the Catholic diocese, the chapel operated for almost a decade, closing in March 1997 after conducting the last Mass on Easter. There were no explanations for the closing of the chapel. The dissenters simply wanted to strike a compromise and agreed by their own volition to send the worshippers back to the Catholic diocese.

What is interesting about this case is the way in which it has divided the Vietnamese American Catholic community as well as the directions in which the different factions wanted to go. In one group, the leadership was advocating self-determination and the preservation of their cultural traditions, practices, and religious worship by creating a place where they could worship in their own language. They also wanted to have a place for the second generation to continue their religious practices. The other group within the Vietnamese Catholic community was more interested in being a part of the Catholic Diocese of San Jose, a movement which may lead to the incorporation or assimilation of the group into the larger American society. That possibility was the fear of the dissenting group. In the end, although the dissenters managed to operate their own chapel for a decade, they were not able to compete against the more established Catholic Diocese. Since Vietnamese Americans have been steadily moving into the middle class, it will be interesting to observe whether there will continue to be a demand for personal parishes in the future or if they will simply continue to attend Masses at the same churches located throughout the city.

ISSUES OF MENTAL HEALTH

The incidence of mental illness among Vietnamese Americans in the United States is surprisingly high. In most Asian societies, mental illness and, by extension, mental patients, are misunderstood and result in prejudice. The general public is frightened and repelled by the notion of mental disturbance. Afflicted individuals are socialized to feel too ashamed or embarrassed to seek professional help. Mental illness, especially the major psychiatric disorders, would bring shame and disgrace to the entire family. If a person's illness became too severe and the family could not help, the person was deemed "crazy" and was taken to a warehouse and confined to isolation from society at large. Minor psychiatric disorders are considered simply part of the human condition. According to Buddha's teaching, life is a "sea of sufferings." The strain and stress of daily living are a normal part of life and the lot of every human being. Each person should learn to cope with his or her individual problems, using his or her own resources, or to accept them with resignation. The individual is not expected to receive external help for minor emotional problems. Most family conflicts are usually handled within the small circle of relatives and friends. Again, the extended family network traditionally occupies this role.

Another cultural problem is the lack of a traditional counselor in Asian societies—one who listens to and advises individuals on how to cope with feelings and problems. Psychiatry is a recent medical field and as such has not reached the mainstream of most Asian societies. As a result of this situation and the cultural taboo regarding mental illness, when a person finally seeks professional psychological help, the conditions are such that they can no longer be hidden or taken care of by the family.

Vietnamese Americans tend to be reluctant to use the forms of mental health treatment and other medical care offered in the United States for other reasons as well. Health service utilization by Southeast Asians is correlated with education and proficiency in the English language. The health care system may be too complicated for a person to understand and to utilize. Furthermore, according to a 1979 report, only 10 percent of sick Vietnamese sought medical care and of those, 73 percent did not return for the required follow up (Silverman, 1979). Rather than choosing medical doctors, some Vietnamese prefer an Asian specialist in acupuncture or herbal medicine. Other factors less obvious but just as important include, for example, working two jobs or more; it is difficult to take time off from work to make an appointment and to visit a doctor during regular visiting hours. A friend or neighbor who serves as the translator may not be available to bring the client to the doctor's office for the appointment. Or the client may not have private transportation and therefore is limited by public transportation.

Beyond the cultural differences, when the Vietnamese refugees first arrived in the United States, there were very few, if any, bilingual or bicultural counselors trained to deal with some of these issues. Finally, there was a tremendous amount of pressure for the Vietnamese refugees to economically assimilate as quickly as possible, their psychological well being and mental health were not seen as high priorities by the federal government. As a result, those individuals who needed treatment upon arrival in order to deal with the difficulties of leaving their country, being separated from their loved ones, being traumatized by the entire refugee experience, or simply in dealing with the adjustment of coming to a new country, did not receive any treatment because of language barriers as well as cultural differences. Moreover, according to Cook and Timberlake (1984), there is a period of adjustment that occurs during the pattern of coping/adaptation. As such, it might not be until eighteen to twenty-four months after his or her initial arrival that the person shows symptoms of having difficulty in adjusting to the immigration process.

Two different categories of mental health issues are found in the Vietnamese American community. The first category has to do with adjustment in the refugee camps. The second category has to do with issues that arise after camp, during and after the process of resettlement into the mainstream society. Although each category is sufficiently distinguished from the other, it is important to note that these mental health problems and issues continue past the time spent in refugee camps and at various times overlap each other.

The mental health problems that are reported to be the highest in the ranking were personal adjustment problems. English language skills, sepa-

ration from families, and war memories are problems normally expected of
migrants that are forced to leave their homeland during a war. In addition,
the lack of money, job skills, childcare services, and transportation problems
is representative of typical problems faced by all refugees and recent immigrants. However, two somewhat unique problems faced by the Vietnamese
refugees are the "survivor-guilt" syndrome and the "Vietnam syndrome." The
survivor-guilt syndrome occurs when a refugee, especially one who has experienced a tremendous amount of trauma while trying to escape Vietnam
and has lost family members but somehow managed to survive, asks why he
or she has survived and not the other members. This creates a tremendous
amount of psychological pressure for the survivor because he or she feels
inadequate and unworthy of living. He or she can imagine hundreds of
reasons why other people were more deserving to live and many reasons why
he or she should have perished.

The "Vietnam syndrome" is a negative attitude toward social participation
in people who are culturally and professionally capable of interaction. This
is especially felt by those who were in the middle of the fighting and did not
know why they had to withdraw or stop fighting during the last month of
the war without having a chance to continue to fight. This syndrome is also
generally experienced by some high-ranking officials who felt guilty about
their military performance during the critical hours of the war and, most
recently, by those who left Vietnam after spending years as prisoners in the
Vietnamese communists' labor camps. While some withdraw from participating in social activities in their daily lives, others choose to concentrate on
working with organizations that can be categorized as "liberation or nationalist organizations." The primary focus of these organizations is the liberation
of Vietnam from the current communist regime. The activities of these organizations are concentrated on demonstrating against the countless atrocities
carried out by the Vietnamese communist government, exposing gross human rights violations, uncovering cruel and inhumane treatment of political
prisoners and religious activists, and the continual protesting of economic
trade between the United States and Vietnam. Even though people inflicted
with the "Vietnam syndrome" have lived in the United States for a long time,
they do not necessarily see the United States as their permanent home.
Rather, they see themselves returning to, and living in, Vietnam when they
finally succeed in overthrowing the current Vietnamese communist government. As a result, most of their free time is occupied with promoting and
achieving this goal.

The second category of mental health issues and problems are those observed after the resettlement period. Vietnamese refugees spent a relatively

short period of time in refugee camps in the United States. Again, the goal of the Dispersion Policy implemented by the federal government was to quickly relocate refugees from refugee camps into the American mainstream to prevent possible negative reactions from the American public as well as to prevent the formation of an ethnic ghetto. The primary problems Vietnamese faced after the initial resettlement period were and continue to be depression, anxiety, marital conflicts, and loss of status, followed by intergenerational conflict and school adjustment problems.

There have been numerous studies on the mental health needs and issues of Vietnamese Americans. The following is a general discussion of research findings. It is meant to be a summary of studies done by psychologists, psychiatrists, and other researchers regarding the general mental health of Vietnamese refugees.

The Vietnamese Americans most at risk were individuals aged between nineteen and thirty-five years. This age category contains both single and married people. As a result of the Dispersion Policy and the primary focus of sponsorship on traditional nuclear families, many single people find themselves excluded from the traditional family-oriented structure, as well as extended family networks. Without the support of the immediate and extended family, single people tend to be rootless. Because they are single, feeling alienated, lonely, and homesick, they have a higher likelihood of becoming "drifters," physically drifting from one community to another—or from one job to another. In addition to experiencing depression, the single people in this age group are reported to experience thought disorders, to inflict violence upon themselves or others, to experience alcoholism, and to feel a sense of helplessness. The lack of interaction and moral support offered by family members, friends, or a community is compounded with the stress and difficulties found in living in a new and unfamiliar country.

Married couples between the ages of nineteen and thirty-five years were most frequently reported to be experiencing family and marital conflicts. Nazli Kibria (1993), a sociologist, argues that as a result of the migration process, many changes have fundamentally challenged and changed the structure of the family. Specifically, Kibria emphasizes three conditions: the high sex ratio of males to females, the challenges posed by the dominant American culture, and the expansion in scope and significance of women's homemaking responsibilities. Young married couples are reported to be acculturating too quickly and seem to have discarded many of the values of their parents and homeland while substituting the perceived value system of young Americans. The lack of employment, or underemployment, and lack of appropriate spouses for young single males was also reported as a critical problem.

The second most frequently reported at-risk age group included those between the ages of 36 and 55 years. Depression and family conflicts were recorded as the two most severe problems. Family conflicts occurred because of the changing role of women. Because of the necessity of Vietnamese to find employment as soon as possible upon arrival to the United States coupled with the lack of English proficiency or appropriate skill level, most people were only able to find low-paying, menial jobs that do not provide long-term stability, medical benefits, or advancement opportunity. Because of the need for two incomes in order to survive economically, it became necessary for women to find employment. This created tension in some families because of the ease with which women were able to find employment in the service or low-skill sectors. Women began to occupy positions that were traditionally held by men, mainly as providers for their families. This resulted in a loss of the husband's traditional role as the primary breadwinner and a role reversal that then led to the increase in family conflicts. However, Kibria points out that although there were challenges in the traditional family structure and gender relations, Vietnamese women remained supportive of some aspects of the traditional family system. The support comes from their appreciation of their precarious economic positions, an appreciation that in turn reinforces their economic dependence upon men. That is, even though women may be earning more money than men, both incomes are seen as necessary to provide the family with a reasonable quality of life. Without two incomes, women would face a difficult time surviving, especially if there are children involved, since women are generally left with the responsibilities of raising the children by themselves. Finally, Vietnamese American women also supported traditional family systems because of the power they would then have over their children as mothers in the future.

Teens aged thirteen to eighteen years experience intergenerational conflicts and school adjustment problems most frequently according to findings from these studies. Intergenerational conflicts include mixed messages given by the society on one hand and those given at home on the other hand. School adjustment problems include the lack of English language skills, cultural differences and differences in expectations, and unfamiliarity with the school system. For example, a Vietnamese child is taught at home not to talk back to an older person and to avoid eye contact as a sign of respect. However, in school, the child is taught and is expected to speak up in class and to make eye contact with the other person involved in the conversation. If young students apply what is taught at school to their family life, they will be seen as disrespectful by their parents. If they do not comply with what is being taught at school, they might suffer academically because they are not following the teacher's instructions. This simple act can create some stress for the child because of the mixing of messages taught at home and at school. Furthermore, since children tend to learn English faster than adults, they might be asked by the parents to help them deal with daily life matters involving English. To the extent that the parents have to rely on their children for these simple tasks, the traditional role between a parent and a child is then reversed. In general, parents serve the expert role because they are adults with knowledge whose responsibilities include teaching the child how to negotiate life's maze. For Vietnamese Americans living in the United States, parents sometimes become dependent upon the child as an interpreter and as a link to the mainstream world. As a result of role reversal, the parental authority and power is quickly eroded. Finally, given the parents' lack of English proficiency, it is unlikely that they can help the children with school work or effectively communicate with school officials about their children's academic standing.

For those over fifty-five years old, depression, isolation, loneliness, loss of family and homeland, and a feeling of helplessness were described as the most prevalent problems. In the traditional Vietnamese culture, as people age they achieve or are granted a higher social status and more respect. These cultural patterns and time-honored customs are oftentimes not transplanted to America. As a result, whereas the elderly held high social status in Vietnam simply because of their accumulation of knowledge resulting from their life experiences and the wisdom they were able to offer to the children, the family, the community, and the society in general, the knowledge they have is no longer seen as useful or practical for life in the United States. In fact, the opposite might be true. Grandparents become dependent upon their grandchildren and their own children for help in negotiating not only the mundane activities involved in daily living but also the many complexities involved in living in large urban settings in the United States.

In addition, for people in this age category, it is significantly more difficult to find employment, let alone work in their former profession or one that is comparable to the level they had in Vietnam. Most of the time, they cannot drive or do not have independent transportation. If they live in large metropolitan areas, in order to use public transportation they must be able to speak some English to ask for directions, or to find their way home in case they find themselves lost in a large city. As a result, the elderly Vietnamese find themselves alone at home with very little to do. Even if they live in an extended family, which includes their children and grandchildren, they are not as needed because their children are at work during the day and have little time for them. The grandchildren are at school for most of the day and, due to the language barrier and the ease with which children learn a new language, it is often difficult for grandparents to communicate with their grandchildren. The elderly experience tremendous loneliness and homesickness in the United States. Churches, temples, and social service centers are the only places where the elderly can socialize with other older Vietnamese.

Within the age group between infant to six years, the most prevalent problem is that of childcare. This results primarily because of the need for both parents to work, the lack of affordable daycare facilities, and the temporary breakdown of the extended family network. The need for both parents to work reflects the fact that most Vietnamese Americans live in large urban centers where the cost of living is generally higher than other parts of the country, and both parents have to work because they are generally not employed in high-paying jobs. The lack of affordable daycare facilities is a problem that most families in which both parents work have to face on a daily basis, regardless of their ethnic background or the length of time they have lived in the United States. The final reason, the breakdown of the extended family network, is the outcome of the federal government sponsorship policy whereby it was thought to be most expedient to minimize the number of people in a household in order to maximize the pool of potential sponsors. Again, the federal government's primary objective was to relocate Vietnamese refugees as quickly as possible.

Finally, children falling into the category between 7 and 12 years of age were reported to have problems with school adjustment. As for those in other age categories, the parents' lack of proficiency in English and the speed with which children acquire a new language play a prominent role in generational difficulties faced by children in this age category. In addition, at this age, there is strong peer pressure from classmates and the mass media to assimilate or to become "Americanized." Faced with this pressure, children this age tend to view their parents' values as backward and incompatible with that of American society. As a result, they may try to assimilate as quickly as possible, which sometimes results in family conflicts over cultural values and traditions.

CONCLUSION

As recent immigrants to the United States, Vietnamese Americans have faced a wide range of social, cultural, economic, and personal issues since their first arrival in 1975. One of the common variables of each of these issues is time. The perceptions of Vietnamese refugees by the American public have changed in the last twenty years. While treated as war refugees from a war which divided the American public upon their arrival, they eventually became citizens. Perhaps they are now seen as Vietnamese Americans or simply as members of another minority group in the United States. One thing that is certain is that Vietnamese Americans are still coping with many of the same issues that were problematic more than twenty years ago. And although the extent to which they have to negotiate these issues might differ because of the development of Vietnamese American communities throughout the United States, they nevertheless have to negotiate them in their daily life in order to become part of the American mosaic.

NOTE

1. Names have been changed to protect the privacy of the individuals profiled here.

4

Employment and Education Trends

EMPLOYMENT

The employment history and socioeconomic adaptation processes of the Vietnamese in America are complex. The complexities stem from four different, yet inter-related variables associated with their backgrounds that impact how each individual is able to adapt to a new life in the United States.

The first issue centers on the degree of urbanization of different Vietnamese immigrants. There is a large variation with respect to the degree of exposure to, and familiarity with, urban life with the arrival of each group. Those who arrived in the earlier wave tended to have lived in urban areas or large cities in Vietnam and therefore were more familiar with the modern lifestyle found in the United States. As in most developing countries, there was a larger concentration of the total population in a few large cities. Conversely, those who arrived in the United States during the second period were not as familiar with urban life, and understandably, had more difficulties adjusting to the many complexities found in a new life in an urban setting.

The second issue in socioeconomic adaptation lies in the difference in levels of exposure to Western culture. Since most Vietnamese lived in either large cities or in the countryside in Vietnam, there is a qualitative difference with respect to how much exposure each individual had to either French, American, or other foreign cultures. Despite the fact that a large number of the total population lived in large cities, only a small number of people had the skills and language proficiency to work for foreign companies. These individuals make up a small, select group of Vietnamese. Nevertheless, a person working for an American company based in Saigon prior to the fall of South Vietnam in 1975 had much more exposure and familiarity with some American cultural values and norms than someone who came from a fishing village off of Ca Mau in the 1980s. This familiarity and exposure might be important variables in later determining the success of an individual's adaptation process. Some Vietnamese refugees had primarily interacted with American soldiers and military personnel, and, therefore, only received exposure to that segment of the United States in Vietnam. Since American soldiers were primarily young men and the military personnel were primarily men, interaction would have been short, simple, and direct.

The third significant issue is the time of arrival in the United States. That is, the year the individual left Vietnam, the period during which they came to the United States, and the specific wave within that period. Again, to reiterate previous discussions, there were many differences in the social, cultural, educational, and economic backgrounds and characteristics of individuals from the different periods. Furthermore, there were also differences in terms of the degree of ethnic community development as well as the level of political and social support from the American public and economic assistance from federal, state, and local governments. In general, those who arrived earlier tended to receive a longer period of assistance from the federal, state, and local governments; those who arrived later, though they received fewer benefits from the government, might have profited more from the already-established Vietnamese American community.

The fourth and final critical background variable is the level of preparation prior to resettlement. In other words, after the initial exodus of Vietnamese refugees in 1975, there were some Vietnamese refugees who had more time to prepare, and perhaps were better prepared than others, for their journey to the United States. The level of preparation could be seen both in terms of English language and labor skills acquisition. If people were planning to escape Vietnam, they might have had the opportunity to attain some skills that they thought might be useful after their resettlement to a new country. Certain skills are more easily transferable to the economy and working conditions of the United States. In general, people who are trained in specific disciplines and practiced as professionals, such as lawyers, doctors, professors, engineers, and teachers have skills that are more difficult to transfer unless they are successful at passing a series of tests to become re-certified. On the other hand, those who had specialized skills such as mechanics, carpenters, electricians, or photographers might more easily adapt these talents to the needs of the American marketplace. In short, there are certain skills that, after some retraining and upgrading, can be used to find jobs more easily.

Despite the aforementioned complexities, the following are some general labor force participation and employment characteristics within the Vietnamese American community. Early studies of Vietnamese refugees in labor force participation rates (the ratio of those who are employed or seeking employment to those who are unemployed, seeking employment, or eligible to seek employment) and employment rates (the ratio of those who are employed to those who are unemployed or seeking employment) were generally optimistic. Bach and Bach (1980) found in a study of pre-1978 arrivals conducted between April and June 1979 that the Vietnamese American labor force participation rate was only slightly lower than the rate for the general population, and that the immigrant employment rate was higher than the rate of the general population. They also found that labor force participation and employment increased steadily with length of residence. In sum, the early arrivals were able to find employment shortly after their arrival. Overall, these jobs were manual labor or jobs in the service sectors and not those offering high pay, stability, or benefits.

For newcomers to a new country, language proficiency is a major factor that prevents refugees from obtaining high-paying jobs or, at least, those jobs that would reflect their former educational and skill level. From among the people who were refugees from the first period, two categories of people surface as they recall their personal circumstances and life experiences while learning English shortly after coming to the United States. The first category includes those who used English to study either a new occupation that did not exist in Vietnam or a continuation and modification of an occupation from Vietnam.

Mr. Dang, a former low-ranking officer in the Navy of the Republic of Vietnam, in his early forties, is currently working as a Certified Public Accountant in an American-owned savings and loan association in Long Beach, California. He recalls:

When I left my sponsor and lived on my own, I got a job as a gas station attendant and went to Los Angeles City College and studied accounting. I don't remember why I chose it but it wasn't extremely difficult. I think my sponsor encouraged me to follow his advice and footsteps. He was also studying for the CPA (Certified Public Accountant) exams. You just have to be diligent and study hard. There were a lot of terms and formulas that I needed to memorize. Once in a while though, you just get a big headache from reading too much.

Since Mr. Dang did not have a specific profession in Vietnam or a set of vocational skills, he was able to choose a new profession that, although he may not like it, was sufficient to provide him with a means to provide for his family. Because he had received some education in Vietnam, he was able to use the community college system and the economic support from the federal and state governments to reestablish himself. He also benefited from a sponsor who not only encouraged him to attend a community college, but also advised him on a profession that he was able to successfully complete.

Mr. Dao, a former diplomat in his mid-forties, owned a legal services office. His practice primarily concentrated on Vietnamese clients and their different legal needs. Although familiar with the English language and himself a law school graduate in Vietnam, he found the two legal systems to be very different. Mr. Dao had a difficult time passing the California bar exam, trying several times before finally succeeding. Before he took the bar exam for the fifth time, he said,

> It's harder and harder for me to study. I am not young. . . . I have a lot of things on my mind. I work full time trying to run this office, I have a family, and then I have to study and try to pass the Bar exam. I can't study the way I used to, you know? Sure law is difficult, but it's the time pressure that gets me. I don't have a lot of time to devote to my studies. I can only study after work and during the weekends. If I was given enough time during the test, I am sure that I can pass it, but here there is a time limit, you have to have the answers immediately, bang, bang, bang.

Mr. Dao typifies a group of Vietnamese immigrants with certain skills and occupations compatible with the United States' economic structure. However, it often takes years to acquire enough English proficiency and the technical language specific to each profession before these examinations can be passed. These examinations are already challenging for native English speakers who were educated in the United States, and therefore they are even more difficult for immigrants for whom English is not their first language and perhaps are older and do not pick up language skills as easily. In the end, some of these individuals give up trying to continue their professions and are forced either to work for lesser wages and prestige or to change professions altogether.

Mr. Tran, a former attorney in Vietnam in his forties, is typical of people from this group. He was not as fortunate as Mr. Dao. Although he also graduated from a law school in Vietnam, he dealt almost exclusively with Vietnamese clients and did not have a strong command of the English language. He also belonged to the Vietnamese generation that was more fluent in French than English. He remembers:

I liked practicing law in Vietnam. It was a lot different from here. It wasn't as structured. At first, when I came here, I wanted to continue with my career in law but my English wasn't good enough. . . . Besides, I couldn't afford to attend a law school; it costs too much. Anyway, I didn't have the patience to study anymore. I didn't have the time to read all these books. I had other things that were more important and which I had to worry about. My wife was still in Vietnam and my energy was spent trying to bring her over here. I needed to work as much as possible to save money to pay for the fees and paperwork.

Mr. Tran abandoned his pursuit of a law career and enrolled in CETA, a government job-training program. He concluded his training in 1980. He then moved to Orange County from Los Angeles and found a job in a small industrial firm as a technician. Unfortunately, he injured his back on the job in 1984 and collected workers' compensation. Despite the difficulties in his professional life, Mr. Tran was more fortunate in his personal life. After years of working to bring his wife to the United States, he was finally reunited with her in 1984. He now lives with his wife and their three children in Orange County, California, and is doing odd jobs to make ends meet while his wife is the primary breadwinner. She works as a seamstress during the week and brings additional work home during the weekend to provide for the family.

The second category of people who came during the first period includes people with occupations and skills that more readily allow for reentry into their former occupations, such as automechanics, welding, carpentry, electrical, and plumbing. Mr. Truong, a former lieutenant in the South Vietnamese Navy, is typical of people in this category. In his late fifties, he is a bus mechanic in Orange County and declares:

I wanted to be a medical doctor in Vietnam when I was younger but was drafted into the Navy. I like working with my hands a great deal and used to work on boats and little things in Vietnam. I was already too old when we got to the United States in 1975, so instead of learning something new and that I didn't know about, I just started to work as a mechanic assistant. It was hard because they [the other mechanics] spoke really fast and had their special tools. Since I could not follow what they were saying, I could not really ask any questions. I had to read a lot of technical manuals to pass an annual re-certification test. It was a struggle but I didn't have a choice. I had my two sons to feed and a family that I wanted to bring over as soon as possible.

After a few years as an assistant mechanic and a lot of hard work, Mr. Truong successfully made the difficult transition to auto mechanic. He was able to find an occupation that he enjoyed and one that did not require strong English skills. His well-paying job also allows him to provide for his two sons and for the possibility to sponsor his wife and daughter. Although able to converse in English when necessary, he is much more comfortable speaking Vietnamese to his family and friends.

The final category includes former white-collar workers such as politicians, soldiers, teachers, and professors, who have found it almost impossible to continue their former careers. These individuals abandoned their former occupations in pursuit of something more marketable, or at least something that will help them find a job. Mrs. Nguyen, a former Junior High School teacher in Vietnam in her mid-fifties did not have the opportunity to continue her career. She reflects:

> I couldn't continue as a teacher in the United States. Who wants a Vietnamese schoolteacher? What would I teach? I had to find something else to do to take care of my family. Although I was receiving AFDC [Aid to Families with Dependent Children], I wanted to find a job. I first worked "under the table" as a cook in a Vietnamese restaurant to save money. It was difficult work and the pay was pretty bad, but we needed the money. Then I got a job as a keypunch operator working for Bank of America in Los Angeles, a job that had to be reported.

Currently, if recent newcomers qualify, they are only eligible for eight months of financial support, a drastic decline from the original three years of support from federal and state governments. The result is such that recent Vietnamese refugees are faced with finding jobs even more rapidly and have little support or choice in learning new skills, which are often necessary in the long run if they want to look for higher paying jobs. Mr. Pham, who arrived in the United States in 1984, describes his work experience and job search upon arrival:

> After three weeks living in the U.S., I got my first job as a cashier on the third shift at a 7-Eleven convenience store in Houston, Texas. I quit this job after four weeks because I was threatened one night by a gunman who tried to rob me. I was really scared and thought I was going to die. I then moved to San Diego, California, and lived with a friend. I was accepted into the Electronic Technician Training Pro-

gram. However, I couldn't find a job after completing the program because I didn't speak English well enough and had no experience in this field. Finally, I got a mechanical assembly job in Santa Barbara, California, through another friend. Then I was hired as an electronic tester on the second shift but was laid off after six months because they moved the company to Mexico.

Mr. Pham represents a group of more recent Vietnamese refugees who has had a difficult time obtaining employment because of the cutback in government assistance for vocational training. Despite the fact that he did not have the necessary skills for entry into a skilled job, he tried to work in several places but had to quit because of the threat to his physical well-being. He then pursued vocational training, but upon completion of the training he could not find employment because his English was not strong enough. Unfortunately, when he finally found an assembler job, his company decided to move their operations elsewhere. This is a typical work cycle for people in the economic sector that requires little skill, offers low wages, does not provide benefits, and offers no stability.

As a general rule, family income increases the longer Vietnamese immigrants spend in the United States. In the twenty years since their first arrival to the United States, Vietnamese have been able to occupy different occupations depending on their educational attainment, job experience, and the length of time spent in America. For example, in 1997, in the heart of Silicon Valley, Santa Clara County, California, which has the second largest concentration of Vietnamese in the United States, there were 1,645 Vietnamese engineers, 478 computer scientists, 289 managers, 2,272 secretaries and administrative support people, 2,472 engineering and science technicians, 1,299 other technicians, and 1,422 assemblers (Freeman, 1997). There are Vietnamese American judges, actors, writers, television journalists and personalities, radio broadcasters, teachers, professors, and elected officials. In addition to working in the high-tech industry, many Vietnamese have also participated in small ethnic enterprises, primarily opening their own businesses.

SERVICE DIRECTORIES AND ASSOCIATIONS

A cursory examination of the 1997 Vietnamese Directory of Northern California, which includes the cities of San Jose, Oakland, San Francisco, Stockton, and Sacramento demonstrates the wide range of businesses and services offered. This eleventh annual directory is 470 pages thick with listings commonly found in the Yellow Pages. The businesses and services listed range from Vietnamese accountants to herbal doctors, security alarms, travel agents, real estate brokers, and the usual listings of lawyers, doctors, dentists, beauty salons, chiropractors, and every service imaginable. The *San Jose Mercury News* conducted a survey and estimate between four and five thousand Vietnamese-owned businesses in Santa Clara County, California.

More than sixty associations are listed in the 1997 Vietnamese Directory. These associations are generally divided into three categories: religious associations including churches and Buddhist temples, professional associations, and mutual assistance associations, including former military units, social services, students, martial arts, refugee assistance, resettlement, and sponsorship.

All of these associations have organized activities for their members and participate in larger community activities. Religious associations provide a place for worship and the conducting of religious celebrations. In the case of the Catholic church, for example, parishioners attend Mass on Sunday, have study sessions after school, provide counseling for people interested in marriage, baptism, and support for people who have lost loved ones. Similar to other Catholic churches, Vietnamese churches also provide Mass for all the traditional Catholic celebrations, including Christmas and Easter. The Buddhist temples provide similar services. Although Buddhists do not attend services regularly, the temples provide a place of gathering for important occasions, including Buddha's birthday, wedding ceremonies, and New Year celebrations.

Professional associations serve the same functions as in the larger society, except their members are Vietnamese. These associations provide professional conferences that serve as a forum where ideas and knowledge are exchanged on a regular basis. By organizing regular conferences, the associations also offer the opportunity for their members to network and to organize regional and local activities. Furthermore, they provide support for individuals who need to inquire about professional matters, including the latest developments in the field, laws and regulations pertaining to their professions, and upcoming events. An example of a Vietnamese professional association is the Vietnamese American Chamber of Commerce of Santa Clara Valley. The organization was founded in 1993 in San Jose, California, by "a group of concerned business owners and professionals who recognized the need to promote business and economic development among Vietnamese Americans and the community at large," as its mission statement proclaims. The organization's primary goal is to promote economic growth and financial prosperity for people in Santa Clara Valley. The Chamber of Commerce provides a wide range of services, including a monthly newsletter, a weekly radio program, business seminars and workshops, and business social mixers and Vietnamese English translation. In general, the organization provides both skills-enhancement workshops and seminars as well as opportunities to increase business for Vietnamese American small business owners. They also organize occasions for Vietnamese and non-Vietnamese business owners to interact with each other. Their members can gain access to the growing Vietnamese American consumer market as well as network with other small businesses and firms in Santa Clara Valley. Although the Vietnamese American Chamber of Commerce of Santa Clara Valley is unique to San Jose, California, Vietnamese American Chambers of Commerce throughout the country provide similar services to their members.

For mutual assistance associations, membership is based on a specific variable. For example, alumni associations from different high schools and colleges in Vietnam have organized banquets and outings for their members to gather and share their experiences as well as to honor some of their former classmates and teachers. The events organized were as small as a single class from a specific school or as large as an entire school. In addition, such events have been organized locally, regionally, and even nationally in some cases. An interesting phenomenon in recent years is the increasing number of high school and college Vietnamese American student associations organizing events for themselves. They have held local and national conferences, banquets, retreats, and New Year celebrations. There is also an annual Vietnamese sports competition organized by Vietnamese American students that draws hundreds of participants from all over the United States and Canada.

There are also more than twenty daily and monthly newspapers and journals written in Vietnamese within the community. These publications are generally free and paid for by advertisements from the numerous Vietnamese businesses. Most businesses subscribe to one or more of available publications. By buying a certain section of a publication, they become regular customers for the publishers. In return, each business receives a designated number of copies of the publications commensurate with their advertising account. Readers are then provided free newspapers and journals as they frequent and shop at these businesses. Although there is not an exact count of the number of journals and newspapers circulated, the estimated number by the publisher of one of the largest daily newspapers is about ten thousand in San Jose and a little more in Orange County. These newspapers are an important part of the community because they allow Vietnamese who have not mastered the English language to keep up with news and events around the country and around their own community. Since the primary audience is Vietnamese, there is also an effort to provide more coverage of news from Vietnam using sources from foreign media, and more recently, the internet. In Vietnamese shopping centers around the country, it is very common to see elderly Vietnamese daily have breakfast, read the free newspaper, and discuss the topic of the day with their compatriots. It has become an important ritual and daily activity for many elderly Vietnamese because they can share their culture and maintain their friendships with other Vietnamese who are in the same situation.

Along with the newspapers and journals, there are countless numbers of books in Vietnamese available for every type of reader, from poetry to politics, from religion to arts, and from traditional Vietnamese to contemporary issues. Some of these books are traditional and classic Vietnamese volumes that have been reissued in the United States for the older generation to read. There are other books translated from classic non-Vietnamese, but primarily French, American, and English literature. There are still other books written to target Vietnamese who want to teach their children Vietnamese or for those who want to learn Vietnamese. Increasingly, there are also numerous books written about the war and refugee experience by some of the Vietnamese refugees themselves.

Although the availability of Vietnamese literature in the form of books and journals outside Vietnam might be seen as a common phenomenon, it is not. This is the first time a larger number of Vietnamese have left their homeland to become refugees living abroad. It might be seen more accurately as a result of their thirst for written materials due to their emphasis on education and the long legacy of war and their displacement. Vietnamese American writers, having witnessed the destitution in their homeland and hostile environment within their lifetime, write copiously. Given the relatively small number of Vietnamese in America, it is quite remarkable to see the proliferation of books available. Indeed, many writers do not write for money or even get paid for their work. They write because they are compelled to do so. They have a story that needs to be told and an audience who is familiar with some of the experiences. Many of the books recount the endless number of sufferings resulting from the war, the end of the war, the escape to the United States, life in the United States, and the consequences of these events on ordinary people. Given the abruptness of their departure resulting from the unpredicted collapsed of Saigon, many felt deprived of what was dearest to their lives. These emotions were exacerbated by coming to a strange country and living among strangers. They do not necessarily miss the material things, or the delicacies, or many other things. Rather, they miss the simplicity, the ordinary activities of daily life, the rooster's crow in the morning, the aroma of food coming from the kitchen, and the slow pace of life.

There is also an emerging group of Vietnamese American writers, those who were educated in the best schools in America, who are now writing articles, poetry, and books about some of the same topics and other subjects as well. This work can be seen as true Vietnamese American literature and, increasingly, Vietnamese American writers have presented their works at professional conferences. Often there is little distinction between the writer, editor, and publisher. It is not uncommon, for example, for the headquarters of a journal or a magazine to be in a garage behind someone's house. There might be a small editorial staff that includes members of the household, friends, and relatives. The cost of printing the book is paid by the writers themselves with little hope of making a great deal of money in return.

EDUCATION

In general, Vietnamese Americans tend to have more education than the general U.S. population. According to the 1990 Bureau of Census Data, 68.5 percent of all Vietnamese Americans twenty-five years old or older have a high school education as compared to 83 percent of the U.S. population. They are, however, less likely to hold a college degree in contrast to the general U.S. population. For Vietnamese American women, of those twenty-five years old or older, 12.2 percent reported having a college education as compared to 23 percent for all women. Vietnamese American men are more comparable to the general population, for those twenty-five years old or older, 22.3 percent reported to have a college education as compared to 23.5 percent for the general population (U.S. Department of Commerce, Census Bureau, 1993). It will be interesting to collect information in the census 2000 project regarding where Vietnamese Americans receive their college education to see whether there is a shift in where they received their college education. As a result of the coming of age of a new generation of Vietnamese Americans, the proportion of those who have received their education here should surpass those who received their college education in Vietnam.

Although Vietnamese American students are a distinct group within the Asian Pacific American students population, they are nevertheless perceived as a monolithic group sharing many of the same general characteristics attributed to Asian Pacific American students. As such, the mainstream American public sees Vietnamese American students as the "model minority"— mainly as intelligent, high achieving, hard working, placing strong emphasis on education, respectful, quiet and obedient, and, finally, successful in the pursuit of higher education. Because of their academic achievements, they have been labeled by the media as "whiz kids" and "super minority" (Newsweek, 1982; Newsweek, 1984; New York Times Magazine, 1986).

However, even while portrayed as the "model minority," Asian Pacific American students are restricted in choice of academic fields. They are primarily seen as excelling only in mathematics, biology, chemistry, physics, computer science, and engineering. Asian American students are seen as not having as well-rounded an education as other students who have mastered other academic fields such as the arts and humanities. As a result of the "model minority" stereotype, Asian Pacific American students in general, and Vietnamese American in particular, have experienced pressure from teachers, parents, other students, and even from themselves, to conform to this image.

In a study of 1,300 Southeast Asian students—Vietnamese, ethnic Chinese, and Laotian students in Boston; Chicago; Houston; Orange County, California; and Seattle—the students' academic achievement was outstanding: 27 percent had an overall grade point average (GPA) in the A range; 52 percent had a GPA in the B range; 17 percent had a GPA in the C range; and only 4 percent had a GPA below a C (Caplan, Whitmore, and Choy, 1989, 1991). The researchers found three primary reasons for Southeast Asian students' success: culturally based values, family lifestyle, and opportunity (Caplan Whitmore, and Choy 1989). Culture-based values are those values that have been brought over from Southeast Asia as core values. The following cultural values were deemed to have contributed to Vietnamese American students' academic success: the past being as important as the present, seeking new experiences, security and comfort, community respect for family, stigma of welfare, sacrifice of the present for the future, balance of work and play, cooperative and harmonious family, perpetuating ancestral lineage, and morality and ethics. Parents are an important variable in living and teaching these cultural values to their children. Southeast Asian parents teach these values in their daily interaction with their children and these values are deeply embedded in their cultures. The more successful the lessons taught, the higher the students' academic achievement.

The second component for their educational success is the students' family lifestyle. Since family is the central institution in Asian life, Caplan, Whitmore, and Choy suggest that there "may be nothing more important than the family's role in instilling, transmitting, and implementing cultural values" (Caplan, Whitmore, and Choy, 1991). Family lifestyle encompasses the important factors of sex-role equality, parent-child involvement, and efficacy. High-achievement students tended to come from more egalitarian families. This is especially true when it came to spousal decision-making processes. In other words, parents from these households tended to equally share decisions regarding family affairs and child rearing. The importance of parent-child involvement to students' achievement is self-evident. The more parents read to the children, review the children's homework, and become involved in all aspects of their children's education, the higher the students' academic achievement. In their study, the authors found that despite their long hours of work, the parents of successful students made an effort to be active in their children's lives. The final factor, efficacy, refers to a person's ability to influence the outcome of a given situation. For parents who believe they have little choice in determining their own job situations, because of changes in the economy, social upheaval, political or military conditions their children's education becomes one place where they can exercise control and have influence on final outcomes. They also see education as a system wherein hard work results proportionately in success. According to their world view, education provides a means for an individual to get ahead in U.S. society. The more educational opportunities the parents can provide for their children, the more the children will excel academically. The stronger the parents belief that they can influence their children's education, the better the children's performance.

The final reason for Southeast Asian students' academic success is their ability to take advantage of available opportunity. Caplan, Whitmore, and Choy argue that even though there were few jobs in the late 1970s and early 1980s when Vietnamese refugees first arrived, they took those jobs that others were not willing to take, even though the work was hard and the pay low. Over time, their unemployment rate declined. One of the key reasons for Vietnamese taking these otherwise undesirable jobs was the belief on the part of parents that their children would have a better life if they were able to provide for them. They were willing to accept low-paying jobs, work hard, and put in long hours because they wanted a better future for their children. Parents encouraged their children to view them as examples of how difficult life is without an education or without a trade to earn a living. Parents often use their life experiences to persuade their children to use education as the main mechanism for achieving success and stability in the United States. However, as a result of their inability to pay for the high cost of a college education, many have sent their children to more affordable public universities unless offered scholarships and financial aid.

Vietnamese American students attending universities and colleges across the United States is a recent phenomenon. A 1990 study examined the undergraduate student experiences of 109 Vietnamese Americans at the University of California, Santa Barbara (UCSB). Instead of simply focusing on

Vietnamese American students at the University of California, Santa Barbara, 1991. Photo courtesy of Hien Duc Do.

their academic success, the study examined the role of culture in the adaptation process, but more importantly, it looked at how students used their understanding of traditional culture, customs, and values to adapt to a new environment; that is, how Vietnamese American students negotiated their roles as refugees and their roles as members of a minority group in a predominantly Euro-American institution.

In general, as newcomers to the university, Vietnamese American students may be expected to operate outside of the mainstream of student culture. However, they come to the campus strongly oriented toward educational success. Of the 109 students studied, 35 percent of Vietnamese American students reported engineering or computer science as their major, as compared to only 8 percent of all students attending UCSB.[1] Men chose engineering as a major more than women by a ratio of 4:1. Engineering has typically been a male-dominated field. What is surprising, however, is that the ratio of women to men is larger for Vietnamese American students: 4:1 as opposed to 8:1 for the overall student body. There is a long-standing Vietnamese cultural expectation, as well as a general societal expectation, that sons will provide financial assistance to their families. There would be more pressure for male students to pursue majors offering immediate monetary rewards upon graduation. In contrast, although women were traditionally encouraged to attend college to obtain a bachelor degree and perhaps additional education, they were not expected to financially support the family in Vietnam. However, perhaps due to financial pressures and the language barrier since their arrival as refugees, Vietnamese American women in the United States are now also expected to provide economic assistance to their families upon graduation. Seventy-five percent of those who major in engineering and computer science are students who arrived in the United States during the second period. Again, this fact should not be surprising since engineering and computer science are among those majors that require the least amount of English proficiency and have traditionally ensured immediate employment after graduation.

Biological sciences is the second most frequently reported major at 19 percent as compared to 12.9 percent for the overall student body. The fact that the two most frequently reported majors are engineering or computer science and biological sciences seems to reflect a certain degree of expectation from the parents. Given the social status of doctors in Vietnam as well as in the United States, we would expect the parents to encourage their children to choose a major that would lead to a profession in the medical field. It was not uncommon during the interviews for the students to report that their parents expected their children to attend college in order to become professionals. In the eyes of the parents, professional careers tend to have more autonomy, provide more freedom, and offer more financial stability. Additionally, the social status and respect accorded to doctors would bring additional accolades to the family.

Business economics was the next most popular major at 15 percent. This statistic is comparable to the overall statistic reported by all students at 16.5 percent. Social sciences as choice of major was next; 12 percent chose psychology, political science, and law and society. This choice rate is lower than the 19.1 percent reported for all university students. Vietnamese American students reporting arts and humanities as their major were similar in number to the overall student body at 9 percent and 7.9 percent respectively. Finally, 10 percent of the students were "undeclared."

The main goal mentioned by Vietnamese American students for attending college was for pre-professional training. With very few exceptions, reasons given for choosing a specific major were pragmatic: the ability to find a job immediately following graduation; parental pressure to choose a "practical" field, and expectations to financially assist and/or support their families after graduation; and minimal English proficiency requirements (engineering and physical sciences vs. humanities and social science disciplines).

English proficiency was especially important among those who came to the United States after 1980. Many students expressed personal frustration and anguish at not being able to achieve their career goals simply because they were not fluent in English, saying that they would rather be poets, writers, social scientists, lawyers, or psychologists, but had to settle for engineering, computer science, or the physical sciences to earn a college degree and perhaps achieve financial security and stability for themselves and their families.

All students, regardless of their length of stay in the United States, mentioned parental pressure to financially help provide for their families after graduation. Pressure came from their families and the Vietnamese American community. Students who arrived after 1980 were constantly reminded of their obligations to their families, many of whom were still living in Vietnam. Since their families sacrificed a great deal to send many of them to the United States to avoid the draft or to offer them the opportunities for a better life, they feel deeply obligated to provide for them in the future. There is sense of guilt associated with their college experience, because they know how difficult life is for their families in Vietnam. There is also an urgency for them to think of their educational experience in terms of short, concrete, and practical goals. Even if they were genuinely interested in a liberal arts education, their purpose for being at the university is to obtain a degree that will help them fulfill their obligations to their families. The university was, therefore, not seen as a place to further their intellectual curiosity or academic challenge.

Put differently, there is a profound tension between the traditional values and beliefs of the old culture and the new environment in which the students find themselves. On one hand, there is the long-standing cultural belief that the scholar should be accorded the highest social position in Vietnamese society. On the other hand, the experience being uprooted, displaced, and brought as refugees to the United States in combination with pressure from their families have led many students to choose fields that offer some immediate financial security upon graduation. At this stage of their developing careers, the welfare of the family seems to outweigh the desire for advanced education. What remains to be seen in the future is whether Vietnamese American students will be satisfied with their choice of careers, or whether they will return to graduate school to pursue and follow the path of the serious scholar.

Graduating from the University of California, Santa Barbara, 1990. Photo courtesy of Hien Duc Do.

CONCLUSION

Research regarding Vietnamese employment indicates that, overall, Vietnamese Americans are doing reasonably well. Those among the first wave of Vietnamese refugees were able to find low-paying jobs because they needed to provide for their families. Those who had employment skills comparable with the American market were able to make the transition easier than those without similar skills. These individuals were able to find employment similar to what they had in Vietnam. Those with professional skills from Vietnam who were unable to continue their professions because they were unable to pass a series of examinations had to abandon their previous careers and seek new skills to find employment.

Vietnamese Americans have also adjusted reasonably well in education. There are reports of success and academic achievements reported by researchers and the mass media. Many are now attending colleges and universities around the country and have contributed to their professional fields. In terms of education, the family was reported to play a particularly important role in this academic achievement process. As in Vietnam, parents emphasize the importance of education and encourage their children to pursue higher education. Although there is a media-influenced perception that Vietnamese American students are succeeding in schools, there is also an important underreported number who are facing difficulties. Individuals from this group need guidance and support to continue their education and to prevent them from getting in trouble with the law. Finally, since the first group of Vietnamese American students primarily pursued professions that required little English, it will be interesting to see whether the upcoming classes will expand their educational goals and professional careers. It is important for the Vietnamese American community to encourage their children to diversify their field of study in order to address all the needs in the community. There is a dire need for linguistically competent and culturally sensitive counselors, teachers, social workers, and countless other professionals to provide services to the less fortunate in the community.

NOTE

1. The data for the overall UCSB student majors was obtained from a report: "University of California, Santa Barbara Fall 1990 Freshman Class ACE Results," Office of Budget and Planning, January 1991.

5

The Impact of Vietnamese Americans

Vietnamese Americans have contributed to the rich American mosaic. In areas with a large Vietnamese American population, they have taken part not only in the development of their own ethnic communities, but also in the communities where they work and live. Four of the most visible ways Vietnamese Americans have impacted U.S. society are festivals, food, the ethnic enclave, and political participation.

HOLIDAYS AND FESTIVALS

One of the many ways in which Vietnamese Americans have contributed to the enriched U.S. society is by sharing their cultural traditions in the celebration of the two most important holidays and festivals in Vietnam: Tet, the New Year Festival, and Tet Trung Thu, the Mid-Autumn Festival.

Tet (Lunar New Year)

The Vietnamese celebrate the New Year on the first day of the first month of the Lunar Calendar. Consequently, the date varies from year but always falls between January 19 and February 20. Traditionally, Tet is the one holiday when everyone in Vietnam, regardless of their social economic background, takes a few days out of the hustle and bustle of daily life to celebrate. It is the time when everyone welcomes the New Year and the return of spring, with its new life and rejuvenation in nature, which is thought to bring a new and happy chapter in human life as well. Each year also brings a new animal

Family attending Tet, San Jose, California, 1997. Photo courtesy of Hien Duc Do.

designated as the year of that animal. There are twelve animals represented in the cycle. They are celebrated in the following twelve-year cycle: Ty, Suu, Dan, Mao, Thin, Tu, Ngo, Mui, Than, Dau, Tuat, and Hoi (rat, water buffalo, tiger, cat, dragon, snake, horse, goat, monkey, rooster, dog, and pig, respectively). A person born in a specific year is believed to share some of the characteristics attributed to that animal. For example, 1997 was the Year of the Water Buffalo, 1998 was the Year of the Tiger, and 1999 was the Year of the Cat.

The celebration officially lasts only for several days, but unofficially, the festivities and activities can continue for as long as ten days and up to several weeks. For Vietnamese, Tet is an occasion for all members of the family to gather together, including those who have deceased. The remembrance of all deceased ancestors is integrated into all the cultural ceremonies during the New Year celebration by setting food and drinks at the altars, burning of clothes and paper money, and worshipping them before the festivities begin. People spend a good deal of time preparing for the event. Traditionally, in Vietnam, one week before Tet, and oftentimes much earlier, houses are washed, all the furniture is cleaned, and the entire house is decorated with colorful flowers and ornaments for the festive occasion. Everyone in the family receives new clothes to be worn during the celebration. Since many visitors are expected, including members of the extended family, friends, relatives, and neighbors, a lot of food is bought and prepared to be consumed during this time.

As with any celebration, food is central to Tet. There are numerous specialty foods prepared for this festive occasion with the most typical being the glutinous rice (*banh chung* and *banh tet*), meat rolls (gio hu), pickled vegetables (dua hanh), and candied fruits (*mut*). Perfumed tea, wine, and rice liquor are common beverages offered along with the specialty foods during this event.

The first official event occurs at midnight of the last day of the lunar year. People celebrate Le Giao Thua, the transition moment, where the old year is bid farewell and the new year is welcomed in with the loud sound of firecrackers, believed to chase away the evil spirits, and the exclaiming of joyous wishes to everyone. An additional important ritual during the first day is the welcoming of the first visitor into one's house. The first person to enter one's house is believed to determine the turn of events that will occur for that house in the next twelve months. Therefore, people are extremely careful not to be that first person entering a house if they are in mourning or are perceived as "unlucky." They do not want to be held responsible for all the bad luck and unfortunate events that might occur in the coming year. Consequently, the first person to enter the house is carefully chosen and only those believed to bring good luck are selected. If good luck and prosperity was brought to the house that year, the same individual is likely to be invited back for the following year. Children are taught and reminded to be on their best behavior during the first few days because parents are quick to point out to them that whatever negative or positive behaviors and actions they participate in during this time period will decide their fate for the rest of the year. As a result, everyone is sure to check their words and actions to avoid bad behaviors during the first week of the new year.

Traditionally, aside from the special food, the Tet celebration would not be complete without three enduring traditions: *li xi* (the giving of good luck money), *mung tuoi* (exchange of new year wishes), and cards and games. As the event symbolizes the beginning of a new and happy chapter in a person's life, people generally extend good will and friendliness to other people. The giving of good luck money is ordinarily directed to children in a small red envelope designated for the occasion. (The color red is seen everywhere during this festive occasion because in most Asian cultures it symbolizes good luck and happiness.) The envelope is not given until after the children have wished the giver, an elder, good health, prosperity, and happiness for the coming new year, which is the most important part of the custom. Included in the red envelope are usually brand-new bills in different denominations set aside especially for the occasion. The amount included in the envelope varies according to the socioeconomic status of the giver and the age and status of the person receiving the envelope. In general, only close family members give generously. The more important point of the custom actually lies in the significance of the act of acknowledging and wishing the elder person good health, prosperity, and happiness. The practice of *mung tuoi*, or the exchange of new year wishes, provides an opportunity for the younger generation to pay respect and tribute to the elderly. Children dressed in their new clothes generally travel with their families to different relatives' houses to wish everyone in the family a prosperous, safe, and happy new year.

Once the formal rituals are observed and all the obligations fulfilled, people turn their attention to entertainment. During the Tet festival Vietnamese engage in many forms of entertainment and social gambling. Card games and other games are played in public places as well as intimate family gatherings. People will often associate the events of the coming year with the results of these games. For example, if one should win large sums of money, it is believed that the coming year will be a financially prosperous year. The person winning at games will be able to look forward to opportunities to amass a fortune. If one loses, it is believed that one will be lucky or successful in other endeavors. These endeavors generally include good fortune in romance, the coming of a child, or other events not associated with financial success. In either case, the outcome is not as important as the act of playing. More importantly, these games provide an opportunity for family members to spend time together and to laugh and enjoy the games. Once the celebration is over, people will resume the activities of their daily life and await the arrival of the next new year festival.

Tet Trung Thu (Mid-Autumn Festival)

Tet Trung Thu or the Mid-Autumn Festival is held on the fifteenth day of the eighth month of the lunar calendar. On this date, the night is often very clear and the moon shines at its fullest. For this reason, the moon on that night is considered to be the most beautiful moon of the year. In ancient times, this night was observed to predict the weather and the events that would affect the crops and impact the lives of farmers and the common people in this agricultural society. Vietnamese folklore has it that if the moon appeared yellow that night, that next year's crop would be plentiful and if the moon was bright and orange that peace would reign in the country. However, if the moon was blue or had a purple ring, people should prepare for the possibility of natural disasters, such as drought, flood, and hurricane that might follow. The festival, with its roots in observing the natural cycle of harvesting crops, serves as a time to relax and enjoy all the hard work and long hours that farmers and others expended while cultivating the land. Over time, the Mid-Autumn festival has evolved into a cultural event shared by all segments of Vietnamese society, but primarily focusing on children. The children are seen as the next generation that will continue the cycle of life in the community. It is also an occasion for everyone to be reminded of the need to take care of the new generations following nature's cycle. On this day adults enjoy the beauty of the full moon while eating a specialty cake called the moon cake (*banh trung thu*) and drinking delicious tea reserved for the occasion. For the children, the highlight of the festival usually occurs at night when they participate in a lantern procession around the village or neighborhood. The lanterns are usually made out of paper and bamboo straws depicting numerous animals, shapes, and designs. They are lit by a single candle set inside. As the children participate in the procession, songs are sung throughout the event.

Celebrations in the United States

Increasingly, wherever the Lunar New Year and Mid-Autumn Festival are held, both have drawn thousands of participants, both Vietnamese Americans and more recently, non-Vietnamese in the United States. Events held in southern and northern California have attracted the attention of the governor, the mayors of the cities in which they are held, members of Congress, and many local politicians, including members of the city council and the county board of supervisors. As the number of people participating in these events increases, corporate sponsorship from those companies wanting to attract Vietnamese American clients and consumers has increased dramatically with the passage of time. Unfortunately, so has the number of unwanted incidents and the need for more police officers to be present. Despite some of the difficulties, Tet and Tet Trung Thu continue to be two yearly occasions during which Vietnamese Americans may showcase their cultural heritage to the larger community and to teach their children two of the most important Vietnamese cultural events that are observed in the United States.

In the past couple of decades an abridged form of the Lunar New Year has been celebrated in the United States. Since the festival is based on the Lunar Calendar, it is generally difficult for people to be able to take time off from work to fully celebrate the New Year the way they did in Vietnam. As such, the festival is generally organized either the weekend before or after the

Celebrating Tet, the Lunar New Year, San Jose, California, 1997. Photo courtesy of Hien Duc Do.

actual date in order to maximize the amount of time to celebrate and to accommodate the largest number of people possible.

For the last sixteen years, a Tet festival has been held at the Santa Clara County Fairground, a spacious, enclosed facility that can accommodate a large number of participants and provide plentiful parking. The proceedings mimic those of other Tet festivals around the country. The festival generally begins with a salute of the Republic of South Vietnam flag and the singing of its national anthem. The saluting of the American flag and singing of the U.S. national anthem then follow. There is generally a few minutes of silence dedicated to all those who have sacrificed themselves to fight for independence and freedom for Vietnam. The customary greetings, speeches, and declarations from local public officials and state representatives are delivered shortly thereafter and their public acknowledgment by the organizing body completes the formal and official beginning of the Tet festival. Although a festive occasion, the festival is also a solemn and painful reminder for Vietnamese Americans since it reinforces the fact that they have lost their country and are a displaced people. For many, it is also a reminder of fond memories they once shared with their families and loved ones, especially if they still have family members currently living in Vietnam. While happy to be celebrating the event in the United States, they also realize that those happy times are now only fading memories.

The celebration lasts three days, and numerous events are organized, most free to the public after the initial entrance fee. Others have limited seating and require people to purchase tickets. The festival can be seen as a combination of a cultural celebration and a business and commercial exhibit. Although there are specific traditional Vietnamese cultural events organized during the festivities, it is also a fair, much like other fairs that are held throughout the year at the fairgrounds.

The cultural activities and events are organized to highlight the rich Vietnamese cultural traditions, including a procession where all the participants dress up in traditional clothes and display cultural customs and practices from long ago in their homeland. There is a hall decorated with all the deities from different religions where people can burn incense, bow and pray, or simply pay homage to their ancestors. This hall serves as a sacred area where Vietnamese can observe the Lunar New Year as they would have in their homeland. There is also the ubiquitous presence of the Lan, or lion dance throughout the festival. Although exactly when this type of dancing began remains unknown, Lan dancing is very popular during the New Year festivals in Vietnam and China.

The Lan dance depicts one of the four sacred symbols (Dragon, Lion, Turtle, and Phoenix) in Asian mythology. As such it is a creature believed to have the appearance of a lion, with its head having one or two horns, a long and graceful body with fish-like scales, and the tail of a water buffalo. The creature is primarily red throughout its body and is believed to be happy and playful. Legend has it that Lan would only appear in times of peace and prosperity or when such a time might be near. Furthermore, for those fortunate enough to see Lan dance, they would enjoy good luck, happiness, knowledge, and longevity for the coming year. Lan dancing is extremely physically demanding and is generally performed by a professional dance troupe that includes many trained members who have devoted countless hours to perfect the moves. The dance involves holding a Lan's head with a long body made out red cloth and supported by one or more dancers in the middle and at the end. The beauty of the dance lies with the performer holding Lan's head while performing a series of moves based on martial arts movements. The more the performers' knowledge of martial arts, the more skillful and animated the dance. Lan dancing is always accompanied by drums and cymbals. The sounds produced by these instruments, along with fire crackers, excite Lan and give it the energy to perform and to be playful. Lan dancing would not be complete without two important mythical legends,

Ong Dia (Earth God) and the Monkey God. Together, members of the dancing troupe hope to bring joy and happiness to people attending the New Year festival.

The festival would not be culturally complete without two other important and popular competitions. One competition is the Thiê´u Nhi Tài Sác, or the Youth Talent Show. The competition is organized by the Van Lang Vietnamese Language Center to promote cultural preservation and to encourage young people to learn and maintain their Vietnamese language and heritage. Competitors range in age from five years to young teenagers living in the Bay Area. The competition includes: traditional Vietnamese clothing and cultural knowledge, a talent show, and several questions posed by teachers in Vietnamese. A panel of judges is selected by the Language Center from the local community. The criteria used are generally based on how well they represent Vietnamese cultural knowledge and the "ideals" characteristics of a young person during the entire competition. Although there is a sense that this event is more a showcase for the Vietnamese Language Center, it is very competitive and the parents take the outcome very seriously.

The other competitive event that regularly draws the most attention at the Tet festival is the Miss Vietnam Tet Pageant. The pageant is ordinarily planned for Saturday night to encourage as many people as possible to attend. Although the event takes place in the largest room possible, it is almost always sold out. Similar to other pageants, there are certain restrictions. The contestant must be a Vietnamese woman aged between eighteen and twenty-six years, never married, never a pageant winner, and a resident of northern California. The Miss Vietnam Tet Pageant panel of judges evaluates the competitors on their ability to speak Vietnamese, on their talents, and on their appearance and clothing. Despite some reservations and criticisms of these events, they both serve as showcases of specific cultural traditions and ideals for the organizers of the competitions. The winner is chosen on her ability to achieve as closely as possible those ideals embedded in a Vietnamese woman.

In addition to the aforementioned cultural events, several exhibit halls display the arts and crafts entered in competitions that have taken place in recent months in order to be included in the festival. The exhibitions include photography, oil and silk paintings, computer graphics, sculpture, floral arrangements, and pottery. There is also space provided at a fee to social service agencies, police and fire departments, local community colleges and universities, city and county government agencies, mutual assistance associations, and other similar organizations to make available their services and literature and to recruit potential clients, new members, and employees.

Vietnamese American volleyball players in a tournament at the Tet Festival, 1993. Photo courtesy of Hien Duc Do.

In order to offset some of the cost of organizing the annual event, organizers have sought corporate sponsorships as well as other ways to facilitate growth and to attract more people to the event in the future. Although successful in bringing some well known corporate sponsors, including AT&T, San Jose Mercury News, Budweiser, MCI, and Blue Shield Insurance, the success has also contributed to the increasing commercialization of the festival. As such, there are several locations throughout the fairground specifically designated for local merchants and sponsoring corporations to showcase their products and services to potential clients and consumers. By purchasing a space at the festival, they can more easily convince the Festival participants of their loyalty and commitment to the Vietnamese American community by serving as proud sponsors for the Tet festival. As the participants stroll in and out of these exhibit areas, merchants and sales people offer them small gifts in the forms of calendars, pens and pencils, magnets, free trials kits, stickers and other small gadgets with their company logos in order to get their attention.

There are also organized sports competitions throughout the entire three-day event, including volleyball, table tennis (Ping Pong), and different martial arts, such as Karate, Tae Kwon Do, and Viet Vo Dao. In addition to receiving trophies, the winners also receive other prizes provided by sponsors.

The celebration would not be complete without food and games. An entire area is reserved for both traditional Vietnamese food and other types of food to be consumed by the many hungry and thirsty visitors. It is not unusual to see vendors at a booth selling traditional Vietnamese food right next to someone selling pizza or hot dogs. In addition to booths operated by professional vendors and restauranteurs, some booths are reserved for the local boy and girl scout troops and student organizations who use the event as a fund-raiser by selling drinks and cotton candy. The organizers also contract with different vendors to provide typical carnival games for children to play. Even though these games may have little or no cultural relevance, they provide opportunities for the younger participants to enjoy themselves. It remains to be seen whether these festivals can sustain themselves in the near future. At least in San Jose, California, in recent years, two small groups have expressed serious concern about the commercialization of the Vietnamese culture and have chosen to organize alternative Tet festivals. The alternative festivals offered were smaller in scale but the programs put more emphasis on traditional Vietnamese customs and practices.

The Mid-Autumn Festival has been organized and presented for the last seven years in San Jose, California. The event takes place at the Guadalupe River Park in downtown San Jose. Unlike the New Year festival, it is only a one-day event. The festival is organized by the Mid-Autumn Festival Committee, a committee overseen by the parent organization, Viet American Forum. They are both nonprofit organizations run by hundreds of volunteers from the community. Similar to the Tet Festival, the Mid-Autumn Festival has also sought sponsorships from the business community and other groups. As a result, there is an increasing number of large corporate sponsors who has donated money and in-kind donations to make the event possible. As a focus of the Festival is on children, the organizing committee has made a conscious effort to not accept donations or sponsorship from companies whose products or services are deemed inappropriate (for example, alcohol, tobacco, or card and games establishments).

The day provides many different activities for parents and children to enjoy and to be active participants in. There are traditional dances and music performed throughout the day on several stages located throughout the park. Since its inception seven years ago, the organizers have been actively and systematically reaching out to other communities in San Jose to share this celebration. As a result, the dances and music performed have been truly multicultural and multiethnic with contributions from other Asian American

Children's pageantry contest, San Jose, California, 1997. Photo courtesy of Hien Duc Do.

communities, European American community, and the Latino community. Since this is a festival for children, there is a variety of events organized specifically for their participation and enjoyment. There are essay and drawing contests, arts and crafts activities organized by local Vietnamese American artists, educational workshops, games, sports, and art exhibits. There is also a formal Children's Costume and Talent Contest similar to the one at the Tet Festival. There are the usual traditional food booths available. The variety of food ranges from traditional Vietnamese dishes to other ethnic dishes, including those from Mexico, Italy, China, and the Philippines. To truly enjoy the flavor of the Mid-Autumn Festival, one must eat the traditional *banh trung thu* or moon cake. It is a moon-shaped cake, made of ingredients such as eggs, green bean paste, lotus seeds paste, mixed nuts, all wrapped in a dough. They are readily available at the local ethnic supermarkets and bakeries during this time of the year. Since the moon cake is relatively sweet, it is best when accompanied by tea.

The culmination of the Mid-Autumn Festival is the lighting of the lantern and the procession that follows. The lantern procession takes place at night when darkness has descended on the city. Before the lighting of the first lantern, there is a formal ceremony to acknowledge and thank all the cor-

Teaching arts and crafts at the annual Mid-Autumn Festival, 1997. Photo courtesy of Hien Duc Do.

porate sponsors, volunteers, and organizations involved in making the event possible. Ensuing are the greetings and salutations from public officials and state representatives. After all the formalities are completed, the attention turns to the Lan dancing that signifies the coming of the long and eagerly awaited lantern procession. There is a large wooden lantern, generally carried by four to six people, that serves as the head of the procession. It is accompanied by the Lan dancing troupes and music. Every child with a lantern is invited to fall in line and to follow along the prescribed route. While everyone is marching, there are traditional songs sung to encourage people along the way. The festival is brought to a formal closure after the procession is completed and good wishes are exchanged by all. Although the Mid-Autumn Festival is a Vietnamese tradition, at least in San Jose, California, the organizers have used the event to introduce this special Vietnamese cultural tradition to the larger community while inviting other communities to share and partake in the celebration of all the young people in the community. The organizers have established a festival that although Vietnamese in origin, has extended to celebrate the importance of all youth in the community. The festival is a call to all members of the community to celebrate and acknowledge the importance of the younger generation and as a reminder to the older generation of the need to provide guidance and support to them.

FOOD

In most large metropolitan areas, Americans have been introduced to Vietnamese restaurants offering a cuisine that is healthy, delicious, and reasonably priced. Vietnamese food has become common and popular in many cities. It is common to find Vietnamese and Americans eating a hot bowl of beef noodle and drinking an ice coffee at the many different noodle houses (*Pho*). Vietnamese restaurants offer a cuisine with a wide range of foods—from food that people eat with their families everyday, such as stir fry vegetables, sweet and sour soup, and salted clay pot fish and shrimp, chicken, or pork, to specialty foods such as the seven-course beef, spring rolls, or a number of seafood specialties. They also provide individual rice plates and noodle bowls for people who do not want to eat family style. One of the other services that some restaurants provide is "*com thang*" or monthly meals. For people who are too busy, single, or do not have the desire to cook, orders can be place monthly (or weekly). The food can either be delivered to the house or picked up daily. The customer can request the quantity and frequency of the order.

ETHNIC ENCLAVE

As a result of the initial refugee resettlement, secondary migration, and continued influx of Vietnamese refugees and immigrants since 1975, Vietnamese Americans have succeeded in establishing communities in urban areas throughout the United States. As is true for many other immigrant groups throughout the history of America, the Vietnamese had to build their own ethnic enclaves from the ground up. These communities were not built overnight and some of the necessary capital did not come from the refugees themselves. For example, the majority of the capital used to build "Little Saigon" in Orange County, California, came from Chinese investors who had connections with ethnic Chinese refugees (Brody, 1987). In addition, for every successful business, there are many others that did not succeed, in fact, many went bankrupt. These established ethnic enclaves serve a variety of needs, including ethnic-specific food, herbal medicines, entertainment (music, videos, soap operas), arts, and literature.

Weekends are when these ethnic enterprises are seen to flourish. For example, on Saturday and Sunday, in San Jose and Westminster, California; Falls Church, Virginia; Fort Worth and Dallas, Texas; Seattle; and Boston, it is common to see full parking lots with many cars waiting to get in. Extended families can be seen eating at any number of restaurants or noodle

Vietnamese American businesses in a strip mall, 1998. Photo courtesy of Hien Duc Do.

shops. Families can also complete their grocery shopping at the market near by. In addition to the regular food, these ethnic markets provide specialty food only found in Asian or Vietnamese markets, including spices, fish sauce, certain vegetables, canned fruits from Asia, pickled vegetables, other sauces, and dried goods. While parents are busy grocery shopping, the children can visit the music and video store to obtain the latest *Paris by Night* video or to buy the latest CD by their favorite singer. The outing continues as the family looks for clothes at the boutiques that offer the latest fashions. In addition to providing these ethnic-specific needs, these community shopping centers and mini-malls provide a social space where Vietnamese Americans who live throughout the local areas, and in some cases from far away, can spend the time to visit with families and friends and get a "taste of home."

POLITICAL PARTICIPATION

Because of their recent history in this country, political participation by Vietnamese Americans is not as well developed as in other and more established racial and ethnic communities. Although there are many groups and segments within the Vietnamese American community, three broad groups

Vietnamese specialty foods, 1998. Photo courtesy of Hien Duc Do.

can be used to present a picture of their political participation. The earlier refugees, as well as the few who had already been living in the United States prior to 1975, had some connections as well as language skills because of their interactions with Americans in Vietnam. They were recruited to work as interpreters, social workers, and orientation workers for those Vietnamese refugees who arrived later. Members of this group have become influential in the community because they were able to learn and understand the American political and government systems while working with American social workers, government officials, and policy makers in resettling other refugees. They later formed mutual assistance associations and competed for resources, such as federal and state funding, to provide direct services to the steadily increasing number of Vietnamese refugees coming to the United States. By and large, this has been the group that has had the most interactions with the outside community and was believed to have a handle on the pulse of the community.

The second important group consists of those individuals and organizations most concerned with social and cultural activities within the community. These individuals and organizations tend to be somewhat politically conservative and are organized in a traditional manner. Many of the leaders of these organizations tend to be from the older generation who are com-

Vietnamese Americans shopping at the supermarket, 1996. Photo courtesy of Hien Duc Do.

fortable with the traditional Vietnamese ways of interacting with the outside world. They are strongly anti-communist and loyal supporters of those claiming to want to liberate Vietnam.

In San Jose, California, such individuals were successful at uniting many different social, professional, political, and military organizations under one umbrella organization called Lien Hoi Nguoi Viet Quoc Gia Bac California (the Association of Vietnamese Organizations of Northern California). They have been the organization that has successfully put on the Tet festivals, the Lunar New Year celebrations. They are influential with the mainstream media about issues of interest to the Vietnamese American community, and they claim to speak for many people because of the many organizations they represent. They expose and report the many atrocities inflicted by the Vietnamese communist government and its countless human rights violations. Their focus is primarily on activities that oppose social and cultural events that they perceive as either friendly or pro-communist. They are very vocal in their opposition and have the ability to successfully organize highly vocal demonstrations in the community.

The most recent event organized by this group is the boycott of the Vietnamese newspaper *Thoi Bao* because they allege the editors and writers of the stories to be communist-friendly. Two controversial events[1] will serve to illustrate the ability to use patriotism as a focal point to organize opposition to unwanted events in the community. The first event involved the appearance of a well-known and popular Vietnamese singer, Thanh Lan. Thanh Lan had been a popular singer for many Vietnamese in the 1970s and up to the fall of Saigon in 1975. Unfortunately, she was unable to escape and remained in Vietnam after the war. In 1994, with the sponsorship of a Vietnamese American and a member of Congress, she received a temporary visa as an artist invited from Vietnam to visit the United States and to perform a series of concerts. As soon as word was received of her possible impending visit, members of this group expressed their belief that she must either be a member of the Vietnamese communist party or be married to a member of the party. The allegations presented were principally based on the fact that, unlike some other artists, she was not jailed after the war for her war-time activities. In fact, she was allowed to continue her singing career and, indeed, had a "good life" in Vietnam. As a result of these allegations and the continued threats of demonstrations, all of the concerts organized for her tour in the United States were canceled with the exception of the one scheduled in San Jose, California. The reasons for the organizers' refusal to cancel the only remaining concert were never revealed. Nevertheless, on the day of the event, there was a large turnout in front of the concert hall hours before the actual concert for a demonstration with a very vocal group objecting to her presence in the community. People who attempted to enter the concert hall were verbally assaulted and felt physically threatened as they walked by the highly emotional and angry demonstrators. The demonstration lasted until late into the night. In the end, despite the willingness of the organizers to take a stand and let the concert take place, the demonstration against her had distraught her so much that Thanh Lan pleaded her case to the audience and only sang a couple of songs. In the course of those several hours, she also revealed that she had in fact sought political asylum earlier that day and was hoping to resettle in America. In effect, the demonstration succeeded at preventing her from performing in the United States. The event had a happy ending as Thanh Lan was later granted political asylum and is now recording and frequently performing at numerous concerts and events in the community. She is once again embraced by many of the same people who had earlier protested her visit.

Another event involved an art exhibit organized by the Smithsonian Traveling Exhibition Service in Washington, D.C., titled *"An Ocean Apart: Contemporary Vietnamese Art from the United States and Vietnam."* This exhibit was seemingly a prestigious event since the San Jose Museum of Art was the only northern California venue chosen for the national tour. The exhibition comprised eighty contemporary works by thirty-four artists, both Vietnamese living in Vietnam and those living in the United States. Although from the same country, members of each group have experienced entirely different life circumstances that have impacted their lives and works. Despite these differences, the exhibit was organized to demonstrate how there are similarities as well. The exhibit was shown in San Jose from May 25 to August 18, 1996.

A year and a half prior to the actual opening of the exhibit, the local organizers of the event wanted to provide opportunities for input from the community and organized a series of "brain-storming" sessions. These sessions included both selected individuals, i.e., those with specific skills, expertise and knowledge about the community, and members of the community at large and elicited suggestions and requests regarding the variety of events to be planned for the exhibit. In addition to the exhibit, there were requests for workshops for children to gain exposure to art, seminars by local experts about Vietnamese and Vietnamese American history, culture, customs, and current issues, poetry contests, and seminars regarding art and literature.

Despite the efforts of the organizers and input received from the community, there was an organized and vocal demonstration against the exhibition's opening. The protesters charged that the exhibition was nothing more than a puppet of the Vietnamese communist government and that the organizers were communist sympathizers. They also encouraged people to boycott the exhibition and all the events associated with it. The exhibition went on as scheduled and the demonstrators disappeared shortly thereafter.

What is interesting about this incident are the reactions from the different segments of the Vietnamese American community and the larger community. By all accounts, *An Ocean Apart* was a complete success. Hundreds of people saw the exhibition and wrote comments and reactions about the artists, their works, and the activities associated with the event. A cursory reading of the hundreds of written comments collected indicate how much everyone thoroughly enjoyed the exhibition. Hundreds of Vietnamese Americans expressed their appreciation for the chance to display the accomplishments and talents of their compatriots. There were no comments regarding the communist propaganda or influence. Although there were comments regarding the Vietnam War and the United States' involvement in it, they were mostly about the appreciation for the freedom people take for granted and those who died fighting to preserve that freedom. Another interesting response came from Vietnamese Americans who sent editorials to the *San Jose Mercury News* during the exhibition declaring their displeasure at the tactics used by the protesters to prevent people from making their own decision regarding the value of the art works. In general, Vietnamese Americans and others were dismayed at the tactics used by the demonstrators, which included verbal assault, labeling, and intimidation, and compared them to tactics used by the Vietnamese communist government to suppress people fighting for their rights and freedom. They challenged the demonstrators to examine their tactics and to live by and follow the rights given to all of us as citizens living in a free and democratic society. Perhaps the reactions indicate the maturity and coming of age of a new generation of Vietnamese Americans more willing to challenge and question the older generation.

The last group of political participants consists of younger Vietnamese Americans who have come of age in the United States. Although not as structurally organized as the two other groups, this group can be seen in many different forums. In the fall of 1990, a group of young Vietnamese Americans, mostly professionals who were educated at U.S. colleges and universities, organized a conference at Stanford University in California, focusing primarily on how to build the Vietnamese American community. Unlike the other two groups, they were concerned with life in the United States and not overly concerned with activities and events taking place in Vietnam. Although not dismissing the importance of the older generation's desire to hold Vietnam accountable for their actions, members of this group wanted to begin a dialogue regarding the future of Vietnamese living in the United States. Since the early 1990s, Vietnamese American university and college students have organized annual conferences at the University of California, Los Angeles, University of California, Irvine, University of Colorado, Boulder, and University of California, Davis. These conferences focus on issues regarding their ethnic and cultural identity, personal and professional responsibilities, and their roles in American society. These groups are consciously trying to create a forum for members of this generation, those who came here at a very young age, are being educated at America's elite colleges and universities, and are intending to stay in the United States, to articulate their ideas, and to implement their vision of how the Vietnamese American community should develop.

NOTE

1. Other demonstrations by this group have included protests against the establishment of a Vietnamese consulate in San Francisco, a display of Vietnamese products for U.S. businesses at the San Francisco Convention Center in 1996, and the Traveling Water Puppet show from Hanoi that performed in Santa Cruz, California, in 1997.

6

Conclusion and Future Prospects

Overall, there is a sense that Vietnamese refugees, and more recent immigrants, despite all the hardships and difficulties, have made it in the United States. For example, the mass media reports the numerous rags-to-riches stories of Vietnamese refugees who came to the United States with nothing and are now wealthy business owners, stories of students who have won spelling bee contests throughout the country, numerous accounts of high school students who graduated as valedictorians in their class, legendary Westpoint military cadets who were invited to speak at the 1984 National Republican convention, outstanding collegiate athletes, multitudes of graduate students who have obtained advance degrees in a variety of academic and professional fields, and professionals who have succeeded and are now moving toward the top of their fields. There are established and thriving Vietnamese American communities throughout the United States. There is even a city in Orange County, California, known simply as "Little Saigon." The one common theme in the success stories is that Vietnamese refugees have overwhelmingly succeeded through hard work, dedication, and family support—cultural values that they brought over from Vietnam. On the other hand, Vietnamese Americans have also been reported as dangerous gang members or troubled juvenile delinquents in the mass media. It has been said that Vietnamese gangs have become the next organized crime unit that the U.S. law enforcement agencies should worry about. In many ways, Vietnamese American immigrants have been either glorified as the "model minority" or demonized as the "yellow peril" in the mass media. These mythical tales of "success" parallel the model minority myth that has also been attributed to other Asian American groups since their first arrival to the United States in 1849. The general perception presented by the mass media is that Vietnamese Americans have now become part of the larger Asian American mix.

Although the future looks generally promising for Vietnamese Americans, the community needs to focus on a number of issues. Among the most important issues are the model minority myth and interethnic relations, economic survival, cultural maintenance and preservation, political participation, and the welfare of elderly and the future of youth in terms of community development.

MYTH OF THE MODEL MINORITY

The model minority image is a label that presents the notion that Asian Americans as a group have succeeded in America. Although seemingly positive on the surface, there are six dangers closely associated with the model minority image. First, the image distorts and fails to acknowledge the differences within the Vietnamese American community. As a group, even though Vietnamese Americans share many cultural characteristics and customs, they are also a diverse group. The diversity lies in the time of their arrivals to the United States, their degree of exposure to Western culture, education, social and economic status in Vietnam, and English proficiency. Then there are considerations of treatment upon arrival and degree of support from social services, family, and the Vietnamese American community. Therefore, Vietnamese Americans should not be seen simply as a monolithic or homogeneous group.

Moreover there is the coming of age of a new generation, those who have been born and raised in the United States as well as the "knee-high" or "1.5" generation. These are Vietnamese Americans who came to America when they were very young and have no recollection of life in Vietnam. Members of this group have grown up or spent the majority of their formative years in the United States. They have gone through the American educational system, mastered the English language, been exposed to American popular culture, and may never have thought of Vietnam as their homeland. In their minds, perhaps, Vietnam is only the "old country," a place far away where their parents and grandparents lived before coming to the United States. It is a place that their parents talk about or dream about, but the country has no significant meaning for their lives in the United States. They may have no interest or desire to ever visit the country. This generation is much more comfortable dealing with the complexities of life in American society than that of the ethnic community.

The second danger stemming from the model minority stereotype lies in the unnecessary tension and antagonism created between Vietnamese Americans and other racial and ethnic minority groups resulting from this image. The model minority myth implicitly and explicitly criticizes other racial and ethnic groups for their own cultural shortcomings by sending the message that in order to succeed, they need to possess similar cultural traits and social values. In other words, if Vietnamese refugees, who came to the United States with nothing and very little support, can succeed, then why are other racial and ethnic groups unable to succeed? The case of Vietnamese refugees is used to make the case that racism is no longer as severe as it once was. The argument is further made that, although not perfect, American society is more open and more egalitarian than in the past. Therefore, if it is not racism that prevents a group from succeeding in American society, then it must be something inherent in a group's culture.

The third danger lies in the racial hierarchy that is explicitly created. Since Asian Americans in general, and Vietnamese Americans in particular, are the "model minority," it means that other racial and ethnic groups are not and are, therefore, lower in the racial hierarchy. This is a dangerous social construction insofar as it might create resentment from other racial and ethnic minority groups. This resentment can easily escalate and lead to social sanctions or physical harm. The mass media has recently reported numerous verbal and physical assaults on Vietnamese Americans. These are *not* isolated incidents, they are indicative of a pattern in the rise of violence against Asian Americans. The following is one of the most brutal and senseless cases of physical violence against a Vietnamese American.

On January 28, 1996, Ly Minh Thien[1] was brutally stabbed to death, the victim of a racially motivated hate crime. Thien lived in Tustin, California, with his parents and a younger brother and sister. He had left his home around 9 PM on the day of his death to go rollerblading at the local high school. He was found dead by the high school janitor on the school's tennis courts the next morning. At the time of his murder, Ly Minh Thien had recently completed a master's degree in physiology and biophysics from Georgetown University after graduating with his bachelor of science degree from the University of California, Los Angeles (UCLA) in 1994. While an undergraduate student there, he was actively involved in UCLA's Vietnamese Student Association and other groups in the community. He was an intelligent, friendly, and outgoing person full of life with a bright future awaiting him. Thien did not know the killers. He happened to be at the wrong place at the wrong time and paid the ultimate price, his young life.

According to the coroner's autopsy report, Thien died of numerous stab wounds to the body, his throat was slashed, and his head had been stomped on. The police had no lead into the killing until a month later when a letter was found describing the murder in graphic detail. The letter had been sent to a former inmate in New Mexico. With this lead and other evidence, the police arrested two young men, Gunner Lindberg, age twenty-one, and Dominic Christopher, age seventeen. Since the time of their arrest, both have confessed to their part in the murder. The *Los Angeles Times* released the content of the letter on March 7, 1996. According to the letter, Lindberg and Christopher had no reason or motive to kill Thien, but did so by stabbing him repeatedly, more than fifty times, kicked him, and watched him die. Although it was ultimately unclear whether this murder was racially motivated, white supremacist paraphernalia were found at both defendants' houses. The letter also included endless racial epithets and hatred directed toward Asian Americans. In their minds, Thien, and others who looked like him were not Americans and therefore it might be acceptable to mistreat them.

The fourth danger of the model minority myth is that it camouflages the continuing existence of racial discrimination in our society by blaming the victim. For anyone aware of current events in American society, it is obvious that racism continues to exist. However, a message often conveyed is that despite all the difficulties and past discrimination faced by Vietnamese refugees when they first arrived, they have overcome them and have been able to thrive. It follows this line of reason, then, that if someone or some groups do not succeed, it is their own fault, or due to their own "culture of poverty," which prevents them from succeeding.

The fifth danger of the model minority image is that, as with any image or stereotype, it deprives members of that group of their individuality. Embedded in the model minority thesis is an implicit assumption of what a person from a specific ethnic background should become. This is especially dangerous for young Vietnamese American students. If a student finds himself or herself deviating from the prescribed image, or not conforming to the stereotype, he or she may not receive support and encouragement from parents, school counselors, or teachers. Therefore, while a student may be interested in pursuing an unconventional career, the opportunity and guidance might not be made available. The student might be encouraged to pursue a more conventional education and career path as prescribed by the stereotype held by the teacher or counselor. An interesting recent phenomenon involves

Vietnamese American professionals who are returning to school to pursue another profession after graduating from college and having worked for a few years. Khanh is one such example. He originally graduated with a bachelor's degree in computer science and worked as a computer scientist for a major computer firm for a couple of years. However, as he continued his professional career in computer science, he realized that his professional interests were not in computer science but in the arts. He decided quit his job and return to school to complete a master of fine arts degree. He is now a performing artist and hopes to become a curator of a museum. There are increasingly more Vietnamese American students who are no longer pursuing careers in law, medicine, engineering, dentistry, or biological sciences but instead are going into careers such as teaching, social work, dance, theater, and research.

The final danger of the model minority myth is that it deprives individuals of necessary social services and monetary support. Since the perception is created by the mass media that Vietnamese Americans are successful and can take care of their own, public policy makers see little need to provide that community with a share of resources. For recent arrivals, the amount of support and social services provided and the length of support from each level of government—federal, state, and local—has steadily, and in some cases, dramatically, decreased. As a result, there is the expectation that they have to take care of themselves more quickly and with less support than those who arrived in the spring of 1975. However, it is difficult to adjust quickly to life in the United States without the initial support of English instruction, skill development, and an opportunity to simply find one's way around a new country. Increasingly, people are turning to family members and the ethnic community for these types of support and find themselves participating more and more in their own ethnic community and less and less with the larger society. Although this might be beneficial for the individuals at first, in the long run, it might be disadvantageous since they will be unable to gain English proficiency adequate to pass the citizenship examination. Without citizenship, they are not eligible to receive social services and, more importantly, are subject to deportation. This has been the concern of many people in the community, especially in the face of all the recent federal and state legislation focusing on welfare reform and the limiting of benefits provided to legal immigrants. The established Vietnamese American community also has many social problems that need to be addressed. As in other communities, there are problems with youth dropout, delinquency and gangs, drugs, mental illness, theft, unemployment, and the elderly. Some evidence of the continuing need for social services are the following. At a recent funeral service of a Vietnamese American youth who died needlessly as a result of gang activities in San Jose, California, a couple of social workers attending the services said that they have attended too many funerals involving young people in recent months. They wanted to find ways and resources to prevent young people from killing each other. In addition, in Santa Clara County, California, for example, an increasing number of Vietnamese Americans have found themselves in trouble with the criminal justice system and are spending time in jail awaiting trial. Furthermore, public defenders have also recently noted that they see an increase in the number of Vietnamese seeking legal counsel from their office. Mr. Sung, a Chinese American social worker in the family court in San Jose, California, has been troubled by the increasing number of reported domestic violence cases in the Asian American community in general and in the Vietnamese American community in particular. Because of the rapid rise in the number of cases in the last five to ten years, there are not enough social workers, interpreters, and attorneys available to help the court in dealing with these issues. The legal representation Vietnamese Americans receive is inadequate and cases are frustratingly drawn out due to the shortage of necessary personnel.

ECONOMIC SURVIVAL

It needs to be understood that for a large number of Vietnamese Americans, economic survival is still the highest priority. The fact that 25.1 percent of all households live below the poverty line as defined by the federal government is indicative of this overarching issue. Even though the poverty rate of Vietnamese Americans tends to decrease over time, 1990 census data lists their poverty rate at 25.7 percent as compared to 14.1 percent for the total Asian Pacific American population, and 13.1 percent for the total United States population. In other words, when compared to other racial and ethnic groups in the country, the poverty rate for Vietnamese Americans is higher than it is for many other groups, and almost twice the national average. This number suggests that although there are some members of the group who have succeeded in obtaining employment, there is a number who has not achieved the same degree of success. Despite having one of the highest poverty rates in the United States, the Vietnamese American poverty rate is lower than the poverty rate for other Southeast Asian groups, mainly, Laotian (34.7 percent), Cambodian (42.6 percent) and Hmong (63.6 percent). Therefore, contrary to the simplicity of the model minority myth and popular belief, the socioeconomic conditions and employment patterns of Vietnamese Americans are complex subjects. These socioeconomic conditions and em-

Van Lang Language Center, San Jose, California, 1997. Photo courtesy of Hien Duc Do.

ployment patterns should be viewed as a continuum. On one side of the continuum are those who have succeeded and are doing well in their chosen professions. On the other side of the continuum, about one-fourth of the total population are still having difficulties and are barely surviving in the United States (Census data, 1990; Hune and Chan, 1997). As the Vietnamese American community continues to develop and grow, this issue must be addressed in order to prevent it from developing into a larger social problem. Community activists, social workers, academics, and educators must continue to bring this issue to the attention of public policy makers and government officials. Furthermore, given that Vietnamese Americans tend to live in large metropolitan areas where the cost of living is generally higher, this issue will continue to be important in the future.

CULTURAL PRESERVATION

As is true for all immigrant groups, the Vietnamese Americans are keenly aware of the need to preserve their culture and ethnic identity. This is a common goal for all members of the community, but it is especially true for the members of elder generation who are greatly concerned with the issue of language preservation, maintenance of cultural values, and ethnic identity. However, while pursuing this goal, there has to be the realization by all concerned that culture is a dynamic process that changes and adapts to new environments. Within the four-thousand-year history of Vietnam, all the many different foreign countries' attempts to change Vietnam culturally did not succeed. This fact should be especially reassuring to the elderly. There are different Vietnamese American organizations around the country that have been pursuing this goal of cultural preservation for a number of years. One such organization is Trung Tam Viet Ngu Van Lang (Van Lang Vietnamese Language Center) in San Jose, California, established in 1982 by a group of Vietnamese volunteers. Most of the volunteers were young Vietnamese American professionals who saw the need and wanted to provide the services. The primary mission of Van Lang Vietnamese Language Center has been to teach and promote the Vietnamese language to those who are interested, including both Vietnamese and non-Vietnamese alike. In order to maximize its limited resources, the center offers courses during the academic school year and only when public schools are in session so that they can use the classrooms on Sundays. This minimizes the costs associated with maintenance and janitorial services. They pay for the use of the classrooms and bathrooms but not for supplies such as chalk and erasers and copying machines.

The Van Lang Vietnamese Language Center operates on a strictly volunteer basis, and students are charged a minimal fee to help offset the rental of the facilities. The tuition fee is $50 per semester, which includes books and handouts for the students. The classes are from 9 AM to noon, with a 15-minute break between two periods and ten minutes before class to sing the old Vietnamese national anthem and to salute the flag of the former Republic of South Vietnam. In addition, as of 1995, each student is required to wear a uniform in the form of a shirt or sweatshirt, which can be purchased from the parent-student association. The total number of students enrolled in 1997 was in excess of one thousand with a staff of more than one hundred, including teachers and clerical support. The youngest student was five years old and most students were junior high, high school, and college age. The classes offered range from level one (elementary or basic) to level 6B (advanced). The courses taught are similar to those taught in Vietnam, with an emphasis on Vietnamese history, geography, and culture. The books developed for the classes have evolved over the years and include linguistic lessons, dictation, and folk stories. Courses are very demanding and the teachers' expectations of the students are high. In order to "graduate" from one level to the next, a student not only has to pass a difficult examination but must also receive the approval of the teacher.

Although the curriculum is successful to some extent, it is also difficult to maintain the students' interests after a few years. They are taught about the kings and emperors, folk legends, stories, history, and geography of a place they do not know. There needs to be a closer link between what the curriculum offers and its relevance to daily life in the United States for the students and their families. At a time when there are many other distractions and peer pressure to conform, it is easy for a student to become discouraged and to lose interest altogether.

There are other organizations, including churches and temples, throughout the country that offer language courses similar to those of the Van Lang Vietnamese Language Center. Judging from the number of students attending these classes and the dedication shown by the parents and teachers, the goal of teaching the young their ancestral language is very important to the Vietnamese American community. What remains to be seen in all these language centers is how long they will be able to maintain their existence and whether their curriculum will be able to evolve to meet the needs of the students and not just those of the parents. As children learn more and more English and use it more frequently in their daily life, it would become increasingly difficult for parents to communicate with their children in Vietnamese, especially if the children no longer use Vietnamese.

POLITICAL AGENDA

Another important development that will take place within and impact the Vietnamese American community over time is the participation of the younger generation in local, state, and national politics. As the younger generation becomes more and more involved in the political process and turns its attention to the development of the community, there will be a shift in focus that generally occurs with the coming of age of a generation. The focus will become the development of the Vietnamese American community in the United States and not devising ways to liberate Vietnam from its current communist government. This process will include issues of political empowerment, coalition building, and interest in local, state, and national politics. For this group, the ethnic community will be a place to interact with people sharing the same issues and concerns.

PROBLEM GENERATIONS AND COMMUNITY DEVELOPMENT

Although the future development of the Vietnamese American community is important, two groups require special attention for the community to be successful: the elderly and the youth. Life is hard for many elderly Vietnamese Americans. As discussed in Chapter 3, elderly Vietnamese Americans face issues of depression, loss of family and homeland, and feelings of helplessness. Because it is difficult for many elderly to learn English at their age, they tend to participate only in Vietnamese activities in proximity to their residence. Members of this group tend to be homebound for a variety of reasons. They do not drive because they cannot pass the driver's license examination or cannot afford the cost of a car and car insurance. They find public transportation too difficult to negotiate because of language barriers and too inconvenient because of the length of time it takes to get from one place to the next. Unlike life in Vietnam, where at least they were able to move about and interact with other people, they are rather confined living in the United States. If they reside with their sons or daughters, the children tend to be busy working to earn a reasonable living in our hectic and demanding society. If there are grandchildren, they are at school for most of the day, and, furthermore, may have difficulty speaking and communicating with them. Since children learn English easier and are likely to not learn or speak Vietnamese, the interactions between the two generations become limited. In 1995, at the Los Angeles airport, several elderly people encountered said they were going back to Vietnam to live by themselves because they thought life was too hard in the United States and they were mentally and emotionally miserable. The weather was too severe in many cases. They never saw their children and they could not talk to their grandchildren. Why would they want to live out their old age in a place where they were not happy? It was their feeling that, although living in Vietnam would be more difficult and at an increased level of poverty, they would be happier and might feel more alive and productive.

For the survival and continued development of the Vietnamese American community, there also has to be a focus on the well-being and future of the young people. According to school counselors and social workers, in the last couple of years, an increasing number of students are dropping out of high school—in many cases before ninth grade. Too many Vietnamese American students are alienated from schools and do not see the value and importance of a good education. In addition to feeling alienated in school, Vietnamese American youth feel they are unable to communicate with the older generation because of language difficulties and cultural differences. They feel as if their parents cannot understand them and what they are going through both in and out of school. This is not simply a generational problem, it is also a language problem. The children cannot speak fluently in Vietnamese, and their parents cannot effectively communicate with them in English.

Group of Vietnamese Americans attending the New Year Parade in San Jose, California, February 1999. Photo courtesy of Akemi Flynn.

They are caught between two seemingly different cultures and are expected to successfully navigate between them without much support. On one hand, there is the cultural expectation of the parents for the children to be more family oriented and to excel in school. They are also expected to learn the intricacies of a culture that is in transition and that might not be easily applied to their daily lives. It is not easy to understand and appreciate the nuances of a culture that has been transformed over thousands of years. Children do not instinctively learn these cultural customs and practices simply because they are born into the family.

They feel that their parents have unfair expectations regarding their professional careers and future choices. The students resented being unfairly compared to their cousins, to the children of their parents' friends, or simply to other more successful Vietnamese Americans whom their parents have read about in the newspapers or have seen on television. To their minds, it is extremely difficult to live up to expectations that one cannot reach, especially when it is not for the lack of trying but because of unrealistic expectations. Now that the older generation has established some economic stability, and since the need for economic survival is not as pressing as when they first arrived, young people need guidance. They need the older generation to provide leadership and guidance in their education and career choices. It is incumbent upon the two generations to work together to provide solutions that are unique to their own community. It is not enough to simply point to all the success stories and assume that Vietnamese American youth are doing well. The community must pay more attention to the needs of youth and guide them in their development to become bicultural, bilingual, or simply to adjust to life in the United States.

There is tremendous pressure from mainstream society for youth to become Americans and to be assimilated. They are bombarded with mass media messages to be "cool" or "hip." They also face peer pressure to be accepted, and to be accepted generally means to be Americanized and current with all the latest fashion and music trends. The youth are not offered a model that allows them to integrate both cultures in order to negotiate the hurdles of everyday life in the United States.

The central question for them to define is "What is it to be a Vietnamese American?" This is a question that is constantly negotiated and shaped by the younger generation as they come of age in a society struggling with itself regarding the notion of multiculturalism and diversity. Youth should be informed that they are not alone in this endeavor, and that there are many Vietnamese American writers, artists, and educators who have articulated the same difficulties of being Vietnamese in America. How successful they are at answering these questions will, in large part, dictate how the Vietnamese American community will continue to develop in the United States.

NOTE

1. For a video on the Thien incident, see *Letters to Thien*, produced by Fusion Pictures (www.accelerated.com/fusion).

Glossary

anh

An older brother; also used as a form of address to an older male.

An trau (betel nut)

Seed from a climbing pepper chewed together with its dried leaves and lime as a stimulant.

ao dai

Traditional dress for women and men.

Bac

Used as a form of address to a person older than one's parents.

banh chung

Specialty dish made from glutinous rice, usually reserved for the New Year.

banh tet

Specialty dish made from glutinous rice, usually reserved for the New Year.

banh trung thu

"Moon cake"; a confection made for and consumed during the Mid-Autumn Festival.

Cao Dai

A minor religion of Vietnam; practitioners are concentrated in the central highlands.

chi

An older sister; also used as a form of address to an older female.

Cho Lon	Chinatown in Vietnam. An area in Saigon where ethnic Chinese lived.
chu	A younger uncle; a man younger than one's father.
Chu Nom	Vietnamese language based on Chinese characters with its own distinct characteristics.
co	A younger aunt; a woman younger than one's father.
com thang	A system for the monthly purchase of prepared food by which people can buy meals from a restaurant each night on a monthly basis. The buyer specifies the number of portions as well as the number of meals per week.
Hieu	Filial piety; this term refers to the idea of love, care, and respect that children give unconditionally to their parents.
Hoa Hao	A minor religion of Vietnam; practitioners are concentrated in the Mekong Delta.
Khong Giao	Confucianism—one of the three main religions in Vietnam prior to Christianity; founded by Confucius in China around 550 B.C.
Lan dance	A dance involving a mythical lion-like creature, usually performed during the New Year and Mid-Autumn Festivals.
Lao Giao	Taoism—one of the three main religions in Vietnam prior to Christianity; founded by Lao Tse in China around 604 B.C.

Le Giao Thua	The moment of transition between the old and new years.
Le propriety	One of the Five Cardinal Virtues that serve as guidelines for being a good person. Demands a person to be polite and civil to other people.
li xi	The giving of good luck money in a small, red envelope during the New Year celebrations.
mung tuoi	The exchanging of New Year wishes.
mut	Candied fruits—a dried and candied, or sweetened food generally consumed during the New Year.
Ngay Gio	The anniversary of a death.
Nghia	Righteousness—one of the Five Cardinal Virtues that serve as guidelines for being a good person.
Nhan	Benevolence or compassion—one of the Five Cardinal Virtues that serve as guidelines for being a good person.
nuoc mam	A flavoring ingredient used in Vietnamese cooking made by the fermentation of fish extract, salt, and water.
Ong Dia	The Earth God—one of the three characters that dance alongside the *Lan* (Lion) and bring good luck to people.
Phat Giao	Buddhism—one of the three main religions of Vietnam prior to Christianity; founded by Siddhartha Gautama in India around 500 B.C.

pho	A dish consisting primarily of noodles, usually eaten in the morning.
Phu	Parents—generally used with Quan and Su to designate the order of respect in society.
quan	King—the person in the highest position in the order of respect in society; the person with the most respect.
quan lai	The mandarinate—in the old system, a body of advisors to the emperor that included two branches: *quan van* and *quan vo.*
quan van	One of two branches of the mandarinate, *quan van* was the civilian mandarinate and was primarily responsible for advising the emperor on internal matters.
quan vo	One of two branches of the mandarinate, *quan vo* was the military mandarinate and was charged with advising the emperor on foreign and military affairs.
Quoc Ngu	Vietnamese national language romanized and developed by Catholic missionaries from Europe.
Su	Teacher—a designation used along with Quan and Phu to designate the order of respect in society; the teacher is the second most respected person after the King.
Tam Giao	The three-religion system practiced by the majority of the Vietnamese people combining Buddhism, Confucianism, and Taoism.
Tet	Vietnamese Lunar New Year celebrated in January or February according to the first day of the first month of the lunar calendar.

Tet Trung Thu	The Mid-Autumn Festival celebrated on the fifteenth day of the eighth month of the lunar calendar.
Thieu Nhi Tai Sac	Youth talent show held during both the New Year and Mid-Autumn Festivals.
Tin	Truthfulness—one of the Five Cardinal Virtues that serve as guidelines for being a good person.
Tri	Wisdom or learning—one of the Five Cardinal Virtues that serve as guidelines for being a good person.
Trung Tam Viet Ngu Van Lang	The Van Lang Vietnamese Language Center, which offers classes in the Vietnamese language and culture.
Viet Cong	South Vietnamese communists.
Xoi	Sticky rice that has been steamed; usually consumed at ceremonies.

Bibliography

Allen, Rebecca, and Harry H. Miller. "Social Organization of Migration: An Analysis of the Uprooting and Flight of Vietnamese Refugees," *International Migration Review* 23 (1985):439–451.

Anderson, Jack, and Dale Van Atta. "Vietnamese Gangs Threaten Compatriots," *The Washington Post*, August 22, 1986.

Arax, Mark. "Lost in L.A.," *Los Angeles Times Magazine*, December 13, 1987.

"Asian-American: A 'Model Minority,' " *Newsweek*, December 6, 1982.

"Asian-Americans: The Drive to Excel," *Newsweek on Campus*, April 1984.

Bach, Robert, and Jennifer B. Bach. "Employment Patterns of Southeast Asian Refugees," *Monthly Labor Review* 103, no. 10 (1980):10–14.

Baldwin, C. Beth. *Patterns of Adjustment: A Second Look at Indochinese Resettlement in Orange County.* Orange County, Calif.: Orange Immigrant and Refugee Planning Center, 1984.

Baudet, Henri. *Paradise on Earth: Some Thoughts on European Images of Non-European Man,* translated by Elizabeth Wentholt. New Haven: Yale University Press, 1965.

Bayer, Florence E. " 'Give me . . . your huddled masses': Anti-Vietnamese Refugee Lore and the 'Image of Limited Good,' " *Western Folklore* 41, no. 4 (1982): 275–291.

Beiser, Morton. "Influences of Time, Ethnicity, and Attachment on Depression in Southeast Asian Refugees," *American Journal of Psychiatry* 145, no. 1 (1988): 46–51.

Brody, Jeffrey. "Vietnamese Car-stereo Thieves Move Like Guerrillas Across U.S.," *The Orange County Register*, October 30, 1985.

———. "Frank Jao: Real-estate and Power Broker," *The Orange County Register*, January 11, 1987.

Brownmiller, S. *Against Our Will: Men, Women and Rape.* New York: Bantam Books, 1975.

Butterfield, Fox. "For Many from Vietnam, Life in U.S. Is Still Hard," *New York Times,* April 7, 1986.

Caplan, Nathan, John K. Whitmore, and Marcella H. Choy. *The Boat People and Achievement in America: A Study of Family Life, Hardwork, and Cultural Values.* Ann Arbor: University of Michigan Press, 1989.

Caplan, Nathan, Marcella H. Choy, and John K. Whitmore. *Children of the Boat People: A Study of Educational Success.* Ann Arbor: University of Michigan Press, 1991.

Capps, Walter. *The Unfinished War: Vietnam and the American Conscience.* Boston: Beacon Press, 1982.

Carrera, John Wilshire. *New Voices: Immigrant Students in U.S. Public Schools.* Boston: National Coalition of Advocates for Students, 1988.

Chan, Sucheng. *Asian American: An Interpretive History.* Boston: Twayne Publishers, 1991.

Chu, Judy. "Indochinese Refugees in America: A Study of Race Relations in America." Paper presented at the Western Conference of the Association of Asian Studies, November 7, 1981.

Conroy, Hilary, and T. S. Miuyakawa, eds. *East Across the Pacific: History and Sociological Studies of Japanese Immigration and Assimilation.* Santa Barbara, Calif.: ABC-Clio, 1972.

Cook, K., and E. Timberlake. "Working with Vietnamese Refugees," *Social Work* 29, no. 2 (1984):108–113.

Crouch, Gregory. "Vietnamese Gangs Tied to Thefts of Computer Chips," *Los Angeles Times,* October 16, 1989.

Daniels, Roger, and Harry Kitano. *American Racism: Exploration of the Nature of Prejudice.* Englewood Cliffs, N.J.: Prentice-Hall, 1970.

Desbarats, Jacqueline. "Ethnic Differences in Adaptation: Sino-Vietnamese Refugees in the United States," *International Migration Review* 20 (1986):405–427.

Do, Hien Duc. "The Formation of a New Refugee Community: The Vietnamese Community in Orange County, California." Unpublished master's thesis. University of California, Santa Barbara, 1988.

———. "The New Outsiders: The Vietnamese Refugee Generation in Higher Education." Ph.D. dissertation. University of California, Santa Barbara, 1994.

———. "The New Outsiders: The Vietnamese American Students in Higher Education." In *Privileging Positions: The Sites of Asian American Studies,* edited by Gary Y. Okihiro, et al. Pullman: Washington State University Press, 1995.

Dollard, John. *Caste and Class in a Southern Town.* New Haven: Yale University Press, 1937.

Du, Phuoc Long Patrick, and Laura Ricard. *The Dream Shattered: Vietnamese Gangs in America.* Boston: Northeastern University Press, 1996.

English, T. J. *Born to Kill: America's Most Notorious Vietnamese Gang, and the Changing Face of Organized Crime*. New York: William Morrow, 1995.

Finnan, Christine. "Community Influences on the Occupational Adaptation of Vietnamese Refugees," *Anthropological Quarterly* 55 (1982):161–169.

Fitzgerald, Frances. *Fire in the Lake: The Vietnamese and the Americans in Vietnam*. Boston: Little, Brown and Co., 1972.

"Fourteen Suspects in Computer Heists Netting $10 Million in Custody," *San Jose Mercury News*, June 5, 1997.

Freeman, James. *Hearts of Sorrow: Vietnamese American Lives*. Palo Alto, Calif.: Stanford University Press, 1989.

———. *Changing Identities: Vietnamese Americans 1975–1995*. Boston: Allyn and Bacon, 1997.

Fry, P. S. "Stress Ideation of Vietnamese Youth in North America," *The Journal of Social Psychology* 125, no. 1 (1984):35–43.

Galvan, Julie A. "Morning of Terror on Creston Lane," *San Jose Mercury News*, September 24, 1995.

Gans, Herbert J. *The Urban Villagers: Group and Class in the Life of Italian Americans*. New York: The Free Press of Flencoe, 1962.

Gilbert, G. M. "Stereotype Persistence and Change among College Students," *Journal of Abnormal and Social Psychology* 46 (1951):245–254.

Gillan, L. "Texans vs. Vietnamese: A Tale of Two Cultures," *Los Angeles Times*, August 20, 1979.

Gold, Steven J. "Mental Health and Illness in Vietnamese Refugees," *The Western Journal of Medicine*, 157, no. 3 (1989):290–294.

Goldman, John J. "Race: The victims may have been mistaken for Korean-Americans whose store was boycotted. The incident follows an appeal to end bigotry," *New York Times*, May 14, 1990.

Gossett, Thomas F. *Race: The History of an Idea in America*. Dallas: Southern Methodist University Press, 1963.

Grant, Bruce. *The Boat People: An "Age" Investigation*. London: Penguin Books, 1979.

Haines, David W. "Patterns in Southeast Asian Refugee Employment: An Appraisal of the Existing Research," *Ethnic Groups* 7(1987):39–63.

———. 1980. "Mismatch in the Resettlement Process: The Vietnamese Family Versus the American Housing Market," *Journal of Refugee Resettlement*, 1, no. 1 (1980):15–19.

Harrison, Laird. "Viet Catholics Plead Case in D.C. 'Abandon Protest,' Mediator Implores," *Asian Week* November 1986.

———. "Bishop Bans Viet Masses," *Asian Week*, December 12, 1986.

Haskins, James. *The New Americans: Vietnamese Boat People*. Hillside, N.J.: Enslow Publishers, 1980.

Henkin, Alan B., and Nguyen Thanh Liem. *Between Two Cultures: The Vietnamese in America*. Saratoga, N.Y.: Century Twenty One Publishing, 1981.

Hoang, G., and R. Erickson. "Guidelines for Providing Medical Care for Southeast Asian Refugees," *Journal of the American Medical Association* 248, no. 6 (1982):710–714.

Horowitz, Helen Lefkowitz. *Campus Life: Undergraduate Cultures from the End of the Eighteenth Century to the Present.* New York: A. A. Knopf, 1987.

Huard, Pierre, and Maurice Durand. *Viet Nam Civilization and Culture.* Ha Noi: Ecole Française D'Extreme Orient, 1956.

Hune, Shirley, and Kenyon Chan. "Special Focus: Asian Pacific American Demographic and Educational Trends," in *Minorities in Education* vol. 15, edited by D. Carter and R. Wilson. Washington, D.C.: American Council on Education, 1997.

Huynh, Dinh Te. *Introduction to Vietnamese Culture.* San Diego: Multifunctional Resource Center, San Diego State University, 1987.

———. *Selected Vietnamese Proverbs.* Oakland, Calif.: Center for International Communication and Development, 1990.

Jamieson, Neil J. *Understanding Vietnam.* Berkeley: University of California Press, 1993.

Jordan, Wintrop D. *White over Black: American Attitudes toward the Negro 1550–1812.* Chapel Hill: University of North Carolina Press, 1968.

Jung, Carolyn. "Vietnamese-Americans set protest of S. J. exhibit," *San Jose Mercury News,* May 30, 1996.

Kaplan, Tracey. "Dispute among Catholics Carries a Vietnamese Flavor in San Jose," *Los Angeles Times,* October 22, 1986.

Karnow, Stanley. *Vietnam: A History.* New York: Viking Press, 1983.

Kelly, Gail Paradise. *From Vietnam to America: A Chronicle of the Vietnamese Immigration to the United States.* Boulder, Colo.: Westview Press, 1977.

Kibria, Nazli. *Family Tightrope: The Changing Lives of Vietnamese Americans.* Princeton, N.J.: Princeton University Press, 1993.

Kirayama, Kasumi K. "Evaluating Effects of the Employment of Vietnamese Refugee Wives on their Family Roles and Mental Health," *California Sociologist* 5, no. 1 (1982):96–110.

Knowles, Louis L., and Kenneth Prewit, eds. *Institutional Racism in the United States.* Englewood Cliffs, N.J.: Prentice Hall, 1969.

Lam, Andrew. "Love, Money, Prison, Sin, Revenge," *Los Angeles Times Magazine,* March 13, 1994.

Landsbaum, Mark, and John Needham. "Four Bandits Raid Wedding Party of Vietnamese in Garden Grove," *Los Angeles Times,* January 3, 1986.

Le, Ngoan. "The Case of the Southeast Asian Refugees: Policy for a Community 'At-Risk.' " In *The State of Asian Pacific America: A Public Policy Report.* Los Angeles: LEAP Asian Pacific American Public Policy Institute and UCLA Asian American Studies Center, 1993.

Levine, Arthur. *When Dreams and Heroes Died: A Portrait of Today's College Student.* San Francisco, Calif.: Jossey-Bass, 1980.

Liu, William T., Maryanne Lamanna, and Alice Murata. *Transition to Nowhere: Vietnamese Refugees in America*. Nashville, Tenn.: Charter House Publishers, 1979.

Matthews, Ellen. *Culture Class*. Chicago: Intercultural Press, 1982.

McFadden, Robert D. "Black Gang Attacks Three Vietnamese in Brooklyn, Hurting One Badly," *New York Times*, May 14, 1990.

McLaughlin, Ken. "Gang Tap 'Nice Kids' Gun Market," *San Jose Mercury News*, September 26, 1993.

McMahon, Robert J. *Major Problems in the History of the Vietnam War*. Lexington, Mass.: D. C. Heath and Co., 1995.

Meinhardt, Kenneth, et al. "Southeast Asian Refugees in the 'Silicon Valley': The Asian Health Assessment Project," *Amerasia Journal* 12, no. 2 (1986): 43–65.

Mineta, Norman Y., Leslie Francis, Patricia Ginger, and Larry Low. "Southeast Asian Refugee Evacuation and Resettlement Program," in William T. Liu, et al., *Transition to Nowhere: Vietnamese Refugees in America*. Nashville, Tenn.: Charter House Publishers, 1979.

Minh, Chi, Ha Van Tan, and Nguyen Tai Thu. *Buddhism in Vietnam*. Ha Noi: The Gioi Publishers, 1993.

Montero, Darrel. *Vietnamese Americans: Patterns of Resettlement and Socioeconomic Adaptation in the United States*. Boulder, Colo.: Westview Press, 1979.

Mowatt, Raoul V., and Bill Romano. "Massive Chip-theft Raids," *San Jose Mercury News*, February 29, 1996.

Murphy, Kim. "Viet Gangs Blamed in Killing of Mother of 14," *Los Angeles Times*, May 8, 1986.

Nakaso, Dan. "Southeast Asian Gangs Spreading Terror," *San Jose Mercury News*, August 8, 1985.

"New Police Effort Targets Asian Gangs," *Providence Journal*, March 7, 1995.

"New Police Effort Targets Asian Gangs," *San Jose Mercury News*, March 7, 1997.

Nguyen, Anh T., and Charles C. Healy. "Factors Affecting Employment and Job Satisfaction of Vietnamese Refugees," *Journal of Employment Counseling* 22(1985): 78–85.

Nguyen, D. "Culture Shock: A Study of Vietnamese Culture and the Concept of Health and Disease," *Journal of the Associates of Vietnamese Medical Professionals in Canada* (1988).

Nguyen, Dinh Hoa. *Language in Vietnamese Society: Some Articles by Nguyen Dinh Hoa*. Carbondale, Ill.: Asia Books, 1980.

———. "Cultural Preservation: What to Preserve and How to Preserve." Paper presented at the Vietnamese American Conference. Stanford, California, 1990.

Nguyen, Manh Hung. "Vietnamese." In *Refugees in the United States: A Reference*

Handbook edited by David Haines. Westport, Conn.: Greenwood Press, 1985.

Nguyen, Hong Kim. "Vietnamese Themes," Paper distributed at the Regional Indochinese Taskforce Workshop. San Diego, CA, 1976.

Nguyen, Huyen Van. *The Ancient Civilization of Vietnam.* 1944. Reprint, Ha Noi: The Gioi Publishers, 1995.

Nicassio, Perry M. "Psychosocial Correlates of Alienation," *Journal of Cross-Cultural Psychology* 14, no. 3(1983): 337–351.

———. "The Psychosocial Adjustment of the Southeast Asian Refugee: An Overview of Empirical Findings and Theoretical Models," *Journal of Cross-Cultural Psychology* 16(1985): 153–173.

Nicassio, M. Perry, and J. Kirby Pate. "An Analysis of Problems of Resettlement of the Indochinese Refugees in the United States," *Social Psychiatry* 19(1985): 135–141.

Ogawa, Dennis, ed. *From Japs to Japanese: The Evolution of Japanese-American Stereotypes.* Berkeley: McCutchan, 1971.

Olsen, Laurie. *Crossing the Schoolhouse Border: Immigrant Students and the California Public Schools.* San Francisco: California Tomorrow, 1988.

O'Malley, Robert. "Vietnamese Fishing Woes Continue: Thirty-boat Fleet Still Not Working," *Sampan* June 15, 1988.

Oster, P. "Indochina Refugees Face Some Resentment in U.S.," *Los Angeles Times*, November 22, 1979.

———. "Texas Town Turns against Refugees," *Los Angeles Times*, November 23, 1979.

———. "Tension between Refugees Other Minorities Simmer," *Los Angeles Times*, November 23, 1979.

Pedraza, Sylvia, and Ruben G. Rumbaut. *Origins and Destinies: Immigration, Race, and Ethnicity in America.* Belmont, Calif.: Wadsworth Publishing Co., 1996.

Perkins, Broderick. "Keeping Up with the Nguyens," *San Jose Mercury News*, June 24, 1995.

Polenberg, Richard. *One Nation Divisible: Race, Class and Ethnicity in the United States since 1938.* New York: Penguin Books, 1980.

Rabaya, Violet. "Filipino Immigration: The Creation of a New Social Problem." In *Roots: An Asian American Reader*, edited by A. Tacjhiki, et al. Los Angeles: UCLA Asian American Studies Center, 1971.

Redick, Liang Tien, and Beverly Wood. "Cross Cultural Problems for Southeast Asian Refugee Minors," *Child Welfare* 61, no. 6(1982): 365–373.

Rohrlich, Ted. "Reputed Viet Gang Leader Gets Probation," *Los Angeles Times*, October 3, 1983.

Rosenfeld, Seth. "Two more in custody for apparent murder-for-hire of reputed Vietnamese organized crime boss," *San Francisco Examiner*, December 11, 1996.

Rosenthal, Rob. *Homeless in Paradise: A Map of the Terrain.* Philadelphia: Temple University Press, 1994.

Rumbaut, Ruben G., and Kenji Ima. "The Adaptation of Southeast Asian Refugee Youth: A Comparative Study." Final Report to the U.S. Department of Health and Human Services. Washington, D.C.: Office of Refugee Resettlement, 1988.

Rutledge, Paul. *The Vietnamese Experience in America.* Bloomington: Indiana University Press, 1992.

Sandmeyer, Elmer Clarence. *The Anti-Chinese Movement in California.* Urbana: University of Illinois Press, 1971.

SarDesai, D. R. *Vietnam: Trials and Tribulations of a Nation.* New Delhi: Promilla & Co., 1988.

Saxton, Alexander. *The Indispensable Enemy: Labor and the Anti-Chinese Movement in California.* Berkeley: University of California Press, 1971.

Schaefer, Richard T., and Sandra L. Schaefer. "Reluctant Welcome: U.S. Responses to the South Vietnamese Refugees," *New Community* 4(1975):366–370.

Schultz, Sandra L. "How Southeast-Asian Refugees in California Adapt to Unfamiliar Health Care Practices," *Health and Social Work*, 7, no. 2(1983):148–156.

Silverman, M. L. "United States health care in cross-cultural perspective: The Vietnamese in Denver." Master's thesis, University of Colorado, Denver, 1979.

Simon, Rita. *Public Opinion and the Immigrant.* Lexington, Mass.: Heath and Company, 1985.

Skinner, Kenneth A. "Vietnamese in America: Diversity in Adaptation," *California Sociologist* 3, no. 32(1980):103–124.

St. Cartmail, Keith. *Exodus China.* Auckland: Heinemann, 1983.

Starr, Paul. "Troubled Waters: Vietnamese Fisherfolk on America's Gulf Coast," *International Migration Review,* 15, no. 1(1980):226–238.

Starr, Paul, and Alden E. Robert. "Attitudes toward Indochinese Refugees: An Empirical Study," *Journal of Refugee Resettlement* 1, no. 1(1981):51–61.

———. "Attitudes toward New Americans: Perceptions of Indo-Chinese in Nine Cities," *Research in Race and Ethnic Relation* 3(1982):165–186.

Stein, Barry N. "Occupational Adjustment of Refugees: The Vietnamese in the United States," *International Migration Review* 13(1979):25–45.

Stern, Lewis M. "Response to Vietnamese Refugees: Surveys of Public Opinion," *Social Work* 26, no. 4(1981):306–311.

Strand, Paul J., and Woodrow Jones, Jr. "Health Service Utilization by Indochinese Refugees," *Medical Care* 221, no. 11(1983): 1089–1098.

———. *Indochinese Refugees in America: Problems of Adaptation and Assimilation.* Chapel Hill, N.C.: Duke University Press, 1985.

Sue, Stanley, and Jennifer Abe. "Predictors of Academic Achievement among Asian American and White Students," College Board Report No. 88–11, 1988.

Sue, Stanley, and Harry Kitano. "Stereotypes as a Measure of Success," *Journal of Social Issues* 29(1973):83–98.

Sue, Stanley, and J. K. Morishima. *The Mental Health of Asian Americans.* San Francisco: Jossey-Bass, 1982.

Sue, Stanley, and Amado Padilla. "Ethnic Minority Issues in the United States: Challenges for the Educational System." In *Beyond Language: Social and Cultural Factors in Schooling Language Minority Students.* Los Angeles, CA: California Office of Bilingual and Bicultural Education, 1986

Sue, Stanley, and Nolan W. S. Zane. "Academic Achievement and Socioemotional Adjustment among Chinese University Students," *Journal of Counseling Psychology* 32, no. 4(1985):570–579.

Suzuki, Robert H. "Education and the Socialization of Asian Americans: A Revisionist Analysis of the Model Minority Thesis," *Amerasia Journal* 4(1977): 23–52.

Sward, Susan. "Arrest in Viet Gang Boss Slaying," *San Francisco Chronicle*, December 7, 1996.

Tai, Hue-Tam Ho. *Vietnam: Essays on History, Culture and Society.* New York: The Asia Society 1985.

Takaki, Ronald. *Strangers from a Different Shore: A History of Asian Americans.* Boston: Little, Brown and Co., 1989.

Thomas, W. I., and J. Znanicke. *The Polish Peasant in Europe and America.* New York: Dover Publications, 1958.

Thuy, Vuong Gia. *Getting to Know the Vietnamese and Their Culture.* New York: Frederick Ungar Publishing Co., 1976.

Time, May 19, 1975.

Toan, Anh. *Phong Tuc Viet Nam: Tu Ban Than den Gia Dinh.* Los Alamitos, Calif.: Nha Xuat Ban Xuan Thu, n.d.

Tran, De. "After loosing lease, Vietnamese school seeks a site," *San Jose Mercury News*, February 8, 1996.

———. "Vietnamese Catholics struggling to reconcile," *San Jose Mercury News*, July 19, 1997.

TranKiem, Luu. "Economic Development Opportunities for Indochinese Refugees in Orange County." Study sponsored by California Community Foundation, 1986.

"Two Vietnamese Students Testify about Friend's Fatal Stabbing. *East/West Magazine*, September 19, 1984.

U.S. Bureau of the Census. Census of Population, 1980.

———. Census of Population, 1990.

U.S. Bureau of the Census. Population profile in the United States. 1993. Washington, D.C: Government Printing Office.

U.S. Commission on Civil Rights. *Civil Rights Issues Facing Asian Americans in the 1990s.* 1992.

————. *Recent Activities against Citizens and Residents of Asian Descent.* Clearing House Publication 88, 1986.

Vietnamese Directory 1997: San Jose, Oakland, San Francisco, Stockton and Sacramento. San Jose, Calif.: Vien Thao Media, 1997.

"Vietnamese Gangs in Florida Rob Patriots, Police Say," *The New York Times*, November 25, 1985.

Vigil, Diego James, and Steve Chong Yun. "Vietnamese Youth Gangs in Southern California," In *Gangs in America*, edited by R. Huff. Newbury Park, Calif.: Sage Publications, 1990.

Wain, Barry. *The Refused: The Agony of the Indochina Refugees.* New York: Simon and Schuster, 1981.

Whitmore, John K. "Chinese from Southeast Asia," in *Refugees in the United States: A Reference Handbook*, edited by David Haines. Westport, Conn.: Greenwood Press, 1985.

Wong, Jan. "Asia Bashing: Bias against Orientals Increases with Rivalry of Nations' Economies," *The Wall Street Journal*, November 28, 1986.

"Young Vietnamese Sentenced to 100 Years for Rape," *Los Angeles Daily Journal*, April 16, 1981.

Index

About the Author

HIEN DUC DO is an Assistant Professor and Chair of the Social Science Department at San Jose State University, San Jose, California. A former refugee from Vietnam, Professor Do has written frequently on Vietnam and Vietnamese Americans.